CONCISE
LINCOLN
LIBRARY

—

EDITED BY RICHARD W. ETULAIN
AND SYLVIA FRANK RODRIGUE

LUCAS E. MOREL

Lincoln and the American Founding

Southern Illinois University Press
Carbondale

Southern Illinois University Press
www.siupress.com

23   22   21   20   4   3   2   1

Support for the publication of this book was provided by the
Class of 1956 Provost's Faculty Development Endowment at
Washington and Lee University.
The Concise Lincoln Library has been made possible in part
through a generous donation by the Leland E. and LaRita
R. Boren Trust.

  Volumes in this series have been published with support
from the Abraham Lincoln Bicentennial Foundation, dedicated to perpetuating and expanding Lincoln's vision for
America and completing America's unfinished work.

Jacket illustration adapted from a painting by Wendy Allen

Library of Congress Cataloging-in-Publication Data
Names: Morel, Lucas E., 1964– author.
Title: Lincoln and the American founding / Lucas E. Morel.
Description: Carbondale : Southern Illinois University
Press, [2020] | Series: Concise Lincoln Library | Includes
bibliographical references and index. | Summary: "This
book is a scholarly introduction for the general reader on
the most important political actors and documents of the
American revolutionary era that shaped Abraham Lincoln's
politics"—Provided by publisher.
Identifiers: LCCN 2019036842 (print) | LCCN 2019036843
(ebook) | ISBN 9780809337859 (cloth)
| ISBN 9780809337866 (ebook)
Subjects: LCSH: Lincoln, Abraham, 1809–1865—Books and
reading. | Lincoln, Abraham, 1809–1865—Political and
social views. | Founding Fathers of the United States. |
United States—History—Revolution, 1775–1783—
Influence. | United States—Politics and government—
1775–1783. | United States—Politics and government—
1783–1865.
Classification: LCC E457.2 .M848 2020 (print)
| LCC E457.2 (ebook) | DDC 973.7092—dc23
LC record available at https://lccn.loc.gov/2019036842
LC ebook record available at https://lccn.loc.gov /2019036843

Printed on recycled paper. ♻

This paper meets the requirements of ANSI/NISO
Z39.48-1992 (Permanence of Paper) ∞

To the memory of
Peter W. Schramm and Roger L. Beckett

CONTENTS

LINCOLN AND THE AMERICAN FOUNDING

INTRODUCTION: LOOKING TO THE PAST FOR THE SAKE OF THE FUTURE

The best guides to understanding Lincoln's political philosophy, next to a close reading of his own speeches and writings, are the principles of the American founding and the political institutions they established. Key among the founders are George Washington and Thomas Jefferson, and the most influential political documents are the Declaration of Independence and the U.S. Constitution. Lincoln also found subsequent political figures useful to his thinking: Henry Clay, Lincoln's professed "beau ideal of a statesman," and Daniel Webster, who championed "Union and liberty, now and forever, one and inseparable," come readily to mind. Even John Quincy Adams, with his devotion to the Declaration of Independence, could be said to have directed Lincoln's attention to important political principles for the looming crises of his day. However, the salient figures and documents of the American founding generation exerted the greatest influence on Lincoln as he addressed the disputes and controversies that threatened to divide the American Union.

For Lincoln, reverence for the American founders was no mere exercise in nostalgia, a trip down memory lane every Fourth of July by succeeding generations to give a collective pat on the back for their association—by blood or citizenship—with a generation who for their time achieved great political ends. Instead, Lincoln believed that the best way to honor the founding was to recognize how much the current generation owed to their achievement, and therefore to be vigilant in their perpetuation of the institutions of self-government. This involved not only handing down the Constitution and laws bequeathed to them but also understanding the principles and practices that inform those political institutions. The prosperity of future generations, what the preamble to the Constitution calls "the blessings of liberty to ourselves and our posterity," depended on this public practice of looking back.[1]

According to Robert Bray, Lincoln read preceptors containing speeches from the American Revolution and the early American republic and consulted several volumes of Thomas Jefferson's *Works*, as well as biographies of George Washington, which contained some of Washington's speeches. Of course, the clearest evidence of Lincoln's familiarity with the founders' writings comes from his own speeches and letters. In addition to Washington and Jefferson, Lincoln cited James Madison as among "those noble fathers" who, while respecting state authority over the institution of slavery, made "no allusion to slavery in the constitution . . . that future generations might not know such a thing ever existed—and that the constitution might yet be a 'national charter of freedom.'"[2] Add to these sources the speeches and writings of the founding era that were in the public domain, from Washington's well-known Farewell Address to Madison's less familiar notes of the debates in the Constitutional Convention, and Lincoln had a fount of wisdom and deliberation about the American regime from which to draw inspiration for the political challenges of his own day.

This book presents the influence of the American founding on Lincoln's politics in a fairly systematic way, with each chapter tracing a particular influence chronologically (for the most part) and drawing heavily on Lincoln's own words rather than secondary sources to demonstrate his reliance on the American founding for his statesmanship. Chapter 1 focuses on the founder par excellence, George Washington, and how his political vision and exemplary character shaped Lincoln's devotion to the union of American states and the liberties to which that union was committed. It also explores Lincoln's frequent appeal to "the fathers" in general and what he thought "those old-time men" should mean to Americans several generations removed from the founding.

Chapter 2 shifts from the founding fathers to the founding document—the Declaration of Independence. The Declaration stands as the most formative influence on Lincoln's political thinking—in particular, his understanding of the connection between the rights of humanity and the purpose of government. Lincoln saw the Declaration as the fundamental charter of American self-government, and his political philosophy comprised key principles such as human equality, individual rights, government by consent of the governed, and the right of revolution. These tenets of Lincoln's political faith also led him to emphasize self-improvement, free labor, and "the right to rise" as necessary implications of the Declaration's account of legitimate government.

Chapter 3 shifts from founding ends to founding means as it explores Lincoln's reverence for the U.S. Constitution and the rule of law by which it secures the liberties of the people. This chapter traces Lincoln's devotion to the Constitution from his days as a Whig Illinois state representative to his tenure as the nation's first Republican president. Lincoln saw the Constitution as a means of securing the ends spelled out in the Declaration of Independence. His respect for the rule of law entailed a respect for the constraints that federalism imposed on efforts to make American practice align more closely with American principle, with slavery in the states constituting the chief contradiction to the "more perfect union" established by the Constitution. Last, Lincoln's constitutionalism entailed an aversion to amending the fundamental law of the land.

Chapter 4 examines what Lincoln learned from the founding generation about how to address the problem of slavery, America's preexisting condition and signal inconsistency with the human equality that formed the basis of the nation's existence. This chapter explores Lincoln's many references to how the founding generation intended slavery to be put on "the course of ultimate extinction" and how this should guide Americans in dealing with the increasingly divisive controversy in the 1850s. It answers the question of why Lincoln insisted he was "naturally anti-slavery" but never called himself an abolitionist. His approach to dealing with slavery within a federal system of government posed an alternative not only to the typical abolitionist demand that Congress ban slavery immediately, whether in territories or states, but also to Stephen A. Douglas's neutral policy of local "popular sovereignty" (or congressional noninterference), to say nothing of the "positive good" school espoused by John Calhoun and his adherents.

Chapter 5 discusses Lincoln's understanding of the original intent of the founders and its relevance to his own times. Although he never used the phrase "original intent," he made frequent reference to "the opinions and policy of our fathers" and similar expressions. While every chapter of this book explores a specific aspect of Lincoln's dependence on the founding fathers, Chapter 5 examines Lincoln's understanding of original intent in general and how Lincoln understood his own reverence for the American founding in light of progress, experience, and the responsibility of succeeding generations to govern themselves.

If there was an abiding political question that Lincoln wrestled with in his public life, it surfaced early in his political career: namely, how to perpetuate self-government. He did not take for granted that the freedom achieved at the founding of the United States would be secure for all future generations. In particular, he did not think doubts about its survival owed chiefly to foreign threats. With prescient insight, Lincoln anticipated that the challenge of perpetuating republican government would come not from abroad but from within. He thought freedom could be lost through its misuse by the citizens themselves and therefore appreciated what the founders had established in terms of principles, practices, and institutions that could help successive generations preserve a self-governing way of life.

In addition, because Lincoln believed that the rights of the people were fixed or rooted in nature, he thought the founders were correct to establish a government that would operate according to principles and mechanisms that were also fixed and not susceptible too readily to change. The modern notion of "a living constitution," which adapts to changes in society through a class of rulers who discern the needs of the people not so much by consent and civic debate but rather by their own expertise and vision, would likely trouble Lincoln. He would have disagreed, for example, with Woodrow Wilson's understanding of self-government as an evolving political apparatus. "That we have come to a new age and a new attitude towards questions of government," Wilson said, "no one can doubt." He thought this new mindset justified "new definitions of constitutional power, new conceptions of legislative object, new schemes of individual and corporate regulation." Wilson believed the founding fathers spoke and acted for only their generation and time, and considered every Fourth of July the occasion "for determining afresh what principles, what forms of power we think most likely to effect our safety and happiness."[3] Unlike Wilson, who believed "each generation must form its own conception of what liberty is" and argued that the Declaration of Independence was applicable only to its time, Lincoln looked back to the founding generation and saw fixed ideals of human nature, civil society, and legitimate government "applicable to all men and all times."[4] Only by reference to these universal principles, and by following the structures deriving from them, he believed, could the rights possessed by all human beings be secured from generation to generation. His constitution was the founders' constitution, which he thought would operate best by remaining as fixed in its restraints on the rulers as the rights they were empowered to protect.

By appealing to the American founding, Lincoln thought he could help Americans of his and subsequent generations preserve the freedom and equality all human beings deserved. In studying his appeal to the founders, one finds both a history lesson and civics lesson of the highest order. Lincoln had to do his history well because he was not the only politician who leaned on the founders for authority on issues of public moment. From his Democratic rival Stephen A. Douglas to South Carolina's secession ordinance to Confederate president Jefferson Davis, a variety of public men and documents cited the founders in support of policies antithetical to those Lincoln proposed. This became most important when the country heard opposing proposals to deal with the growing agitation over the future of slavery in America, most of which claimed support from the founders. The lesson from Lincoln was that getting the founders right would not only get America right during his time but also point the way to lasting freedom for the rest of the world. This book was written in hopes that Lincoln's lessons from the American founding still hold true today.

LINCOLN, GEORGE WASHINGTON, AND THE FOUNDING FATHERS: AN APPEAL TO THE FOUNDER PAR EXCELLENCE

> Washington is the mightiest name of earth—long since mightiest in the cause of civil liberty; still mightiest in moral reformation.
>
> —Abraham Lincoln, Temperance Address (1842)

As American founders go, George Washington stands as the only "indispensable man" of the American Revolution. As commander in chief of the Continental Army from 1775 to 1783, Washington led a ragtag assemblage of American colonists in their fight to establish a separate nation from mother England. Even before independence was achieved, Washington was becoming known as "the father of his country." In 1777, General Henry Knox wrote to Washington to say that "the people of America look up to you as their Father and into your hands they intrust their *all* fully, confident of every exertion on your part for their security and happiness."[1] After resigning his military commission to the Second Continental Congress in December 1783, Washington later returned to preside over the Constitutional Convention of 1787, which produced a national government that most Americans expected would employ his services yet again. He became the only president elected unanimously to the office (twice). When he refused to stand for election to a third term,

Washington cemented his reputation as America's public servant par excellence and was eulogized by Lord Byron as "the Cincinnatus of the West."[2] His long-standing and farsighted efforts to forge a nation out of the struggle for independence made Washington *the* founding father—the man without whom no United States would have been born—and from whom "Father Abraham" drew inspiration to become the savior of the American union.

Early in his political career, Lincoln used a lecture to young professionals in Springfield, Illinois, to reflect on the longevity of the American experiment in self-government and potential threats to its perpetuation. In doing so, he evaluated the achievement of Washington and the founding generation in establishing the American republic. One likely source for Lincoln's musings was a June 17, 1825, speech by Daniel Webster, who delivered it at the laying of a cornerstone of a monument to the Battle of Bunker Hill. Webster hoped the monument would "foster a constant regard for the principles of the Revolution." In 1838, Webster's speech prompted Lincoln to consider the role of public memory in maintaining free government. Whereas Webster was fairly sanguine about "popular governments" being "as durable and permanent as other systems," Lincoln was not so sure. Like Webster, who noted that those "who established our liberty and our government are daily dropping from among us," Lincoln observed that this "*living history*" once "found in every family" was now gone and could no longer serve as a living reminder of the cost of free government. He therefore devoted most of his 1838 speech, titled "On the Perpetuation of Our Political Institutions," to explaining the new challenges posed by a self-governing society that no longer had living testimonies to the American Revolution.[3]

Lincoln esteemed the work of the founders in establishing a system of government that secured "the ends of civil and religious liberty" better than any the world had ever known. He thought that his generation owed them a debt of gratitude for this achievement and could fulfill that obligation by maintaining that form of government and passing it on to the next generation. Lincoln said this was just toward themselves, something they owed their own posterity, and an act of love "for our species." He praised American government not simply because it was his government but also because it was good. He also praised his forebears for their efforts in erecting "a political edifice of liberty and equal rights," adding, "and nobly they performed it."[4]

But Lincoln's appraisal of the founders contained some qualifications. Despite their noteworthy achievement, he candidly noted that the successful perpetuation of the government "in its original form" until his day was "not much to be wondered at." The government "had many props to support it through that period" that no longer existed. The novelty of the American experiment in self-government gave the founding generation a grand incentive: If they succeeded, "they were to be immortalized." Had they failed, their attempt to establish a viable republic "before an admiring world" would have drawn ridicule and infamy for only a "fleeting hour." Thus, Lincoln depicted the American founding as a low-risk, high-reward proposition, especially for any who "sought celebrity and fame, and distinction." He implied that those who sought glory would have more incentive to make a name for themselves by making America successful than by defending the old regime. While this was not a direct criticism of any of the founders, it dimmed the luster of their achievement by admitting the possibility of more self-interested motives as supplemental supports in the struggle for independence.[5]

Lincoln highlighted the ambition for glory to indicate how it contributed to the founding's success but could do so no longer. This situation was now likely to do more harm than good, given that founding a new nation—especially a nation that demonstrated that human beings could rule themselves—was no longer a possibility for "men of ambition and talents." While there are many founders of nations, there can be only one founder of the first successful self-governing nation. The American founders, and Washington in particular, got there first. Even Webster acknowledged, "We can win no laurels in a war for independence. Earlier and worthier hands have gathered them all." He added, "Nor are there places for us by the side of Solon, and Alfred, and other founders of states. Our fathers have filled them." Webster concluded that what was left for subsequent generations was the "defence and preservation" of the work of their ancestors, which should make "improvement" the watchword of their generation. If founding was off the table for ambitious souls, then "let us advance the arts of peace and the works of peace." In short, those seeking to do "something worthy to be remembered" would have to content themselves not with founding but with building on what was already founded—that is, developing the resources of a self-governing and peaceful nation.[6]

Lincoln parted with Webster at this point by lingering on the problem of those few individuals who sought the glory of "an Alexander, a Caesar, or a Napoleon." He observed ominously that "with the catching, end the pleasures of the chase." Those most ambitious for fame would not be satisfied with supporting the work of predecessors. "Towering genius," Lincoln declared, "sees *no distinction* in adding story to story, upon the monuments of fame, erected to the memory of others." Their hunger for glory would be satisfied only through some great political action that set them apart from other great men, "whether at the expense of emancipating slaves, or enslaving freemen." If they could not build "a political edifice of liberty and equal rights," they would achieve fame by wrecking it.[7]

Lincoln also explained another threat to the perpetuation of self-government: "the jealousy, envy, and avarice, incident to our nature," along with "the deep rooted principles of *hate*, and the powerful motive of *revenge*." During the Revolution, these were "in a great measure smothered and rendered inactive" or, "instead of being turned against each other, were directed exclusively against the British nation." Lincoln concluded that "from the force of circumstances, the basest principles of our nature, were either made to lie dormant, or to become the active agents in the advancement of the noblest of causes—that of establishing and maintaining civil and religious liberty." For subsequent generations of Americans to enjoy the fruit of liberty, these less savory aspects of human nature would require the citizenry to develop a different capacity of their nature—namely, a character marked by "reverence for the laws," which Lincoln argued was necessary in an era where mobs seemed to be on the rise.[8]

By implication, George Washington's work as a founder was somewhat easier than the task of keeping the nation together in later years. Lincoln assumed a greater degree of unity among the colonists than today's historians are willing to grant. Still, his main point was that the task of perpetuating self-government faced dangers that did not exist at the time of the founding. This new danger required a new solution, which ran counter to what Daniel Webster proposed in 1825.

Webster said that the Bunker Hill Monument would stand as a reminder to later generations of "the value and importance of the achievements of our ancestors." He differed from Lincoln about how to stir that memory: "Human beings are composed, not of reason only, but of imagination also, and sentiment." Where Webster appealed to the heart, Lincoln appealed to the mind: "Reason, cold, calculating, unimpassioned reason, must furnish all the materials for our future support and defence." Early in his 1838 speech, Lincoln called attention to "the increasing disregard for law which pervades the country," as mobs sought to enforce justice in the streets instead of trusting the slow, deliberate processes of courts. He believed that the passions of the many could become manipulated by those few who sought to make their name on the ruins of free government. Whether the passions of the multitude who sought justice at the local level or the "ruling passion" of the few who sought glory on a grand scale, Lincoln concluded, "Passion has helped us; but can do so no more. It will in future be our enemy." Despite justice being their aim, the passions of the founding period, "directed exclusively against the British nation," had become destructive forces of impatience and indignation.[9] When Webster proclaimed, "The last hopes of mankind . . . rest with us," he foreshadowed Lincoln's wartime praise of America as "the last best, hope of earth." Both men saw the success of popular government in the success of America. Nevertheless, Lincoln saw a greater need to emphasize "sober reason" rather than "sentiments" and "feeling" as the key to the perpetuation of self-government. Needless to say, he employed reason in this early speech to give the warning and point the way to a more secure future for succeeding generations of Americans.[10]

Nevertheless, Lincoln expressed his own fidelity to the achievements of the founders by concluding his speech with a tribute to Washington: "that we improved to the last; that we remained free to the last; that we revered his name to the last; that, during his long sleep, we permitted no hostile foot to pass over or desecrate his resting place; shall be that which to learn the last trump shall awaken our WASHINGTON." Remaining "free to the last" would be the product of a people who accepted Lincoln's solution to the problem of mob violence and those "towering geniuses" who would exploit a disaffected populace to achieve glory. Lincoln cited Washington as the leader of a founding generation that was committed to establishing a regime devoted to freedom but that entailed a self-imposed restraint as necessary to ensure the enjoyment of freedom. In addition, during the Civil War, Lincoln would praise Washington and the founders in general for establishing a union of American states and the free institutions that subsequent generations had so far enjoyed: "May our children and our children's children to a thousand generations, continue to enjoy the benefits conferred upon us by a united country, and have cause yet to rejoice under those glorious institutions bequeathed us by Washington and his compeers." In sum, Lincoln wanted his generation of Americans to make Washington proud by perpetuating what Washington's generation began.[11]

When he traveled to his first inauguration as president, he noted the early impression Washington's life made on him. Lincoln stopped at Trenton, New Jersey, the state capital and site of Washington's famous surprise attack on the Hessians after his legendary crossing of the Delaware River on Christmas night. "In the early Revolutionary struggle," Lincoln observed, "few of the States among the old Thirteen had more of the battle-fields of the country within their limits than old New-Jersey. May I be pardoned if, upon this occasion, I mention that away back in my childhood, the earliest days of my being able to read, I got hold of a small book, such a one as few of the younger members have ever seen, 'Weem's Life of Washington.'" Lincoln credited the biography by Parson Weems, famous for its concocted story of Washington confessing to chopping down a cherry tree, for introducing him to "the battle fields and struggles for the liberties of the country." He added that "none fixed themselves upon my imagination so deeply as the struggle here at Trenton, New-Jersey. The crossing of the river; the contest with the Hessians; the great hardships endured at that time, all fixed themselves on my memory more than any single revolutionary event."[12]

But the story of American bravery and resolution inspired by Washington's leadership moved Lincoln, "boy even though I was," to imagine "something more than common that those men struggled for." Lincoln repeated the word *struggle* several times in his brief remarks before the New Jersey Senate on February 21, 1861, and left his audience in suspense as to the object of that struggle: "I am exceedingly anxious that that thing which they struggled for; that something even more than National Independence; that something that held out a great promise to all the people of the world to all time to come." What could be worth all that effort, that mighty struggle of that generation of Americans? With the United States in the process of disuniting, Lincoln sought to connect his forthcoming service as president to the work of the founders, as well as efforts of fellow citizens to preserve the American union from her domestic foes. He did so by finally revealing the reason for the struggle: "I am exceedingly anxious that this Union, the Constitution, and the liberties of the people shall be perpetuated in accordance with the original idea for which that struggle was made, and I shall be most happy indeed if I shall be an humble instrument in the hands of the Almighty, and of this, his almost chosen people, for perpetuating the object of that great struggle." He committed himself to perpetuating the union of the American states, a constitution that helped perfect that union, and the aim of those political structures—"the liberties of the people"—in a manner consistent with the grand purpose that gave birth to the American nation.[13]

That grand purpose, what Lincoln called "a great promise," was what he paraphrased from the Declaration of Independence the following day in Philadelphia: that "which gave promise that in due time the weights should be lifted from the shoulders of all men, and that *all* should have an equal chance." Even more than what he called "the mere matter of the separation of the colonies from the mother land" was "something in that Declaration giving liberty, not alone to the people of this country, but hope to the world for all future time." As he made his way to the nation's capital, Lincoln used these brief speeches to call for not only the preservation of the American union but also the preservation of its original reason for declaring independence: that its citizens could govern themselves according to the universal principle of human equality and individual rights. Acknowledging that this idea would take time to come to fruition, Lincoln maintained that this "promise" was what "kept this Confederacy so long together" through the Revolutionary War period. It was that which made "the toils that were endured by the officers and soldiers of the army, who achieved that Independence" worth the struggle. The chief officer, of course, was Commander in Chief George Washington.[14]

On the day Lincoln departed his hometown of Springfield, Illinois, to travel to the nation's capital for his inauguration as president, he gave an impromptu speech to the gathered throng of well-wishers. He devoted most of his brief remarks to a reflection on his presidential task in light of Washington's as a founder: "I now leave, not knowing when, or whether ever, I may return, with a task before me greater than that which rested upon Washington." Lincoln observed that his task—which went unmentioned but which his audience knew was nothing less than the preservation of the American union—was "greater" than Washington's, which was to establish the American union. Both were daunting undertakings. By comparing the two, Lincoln invited his audience not only to appreciate the challenge he faced but also to consider why his task was more difficult than Washington's. If both could be said to be unifiers of the American people, why did Lincoln believe preserving the union of American states would prove more difficult than unifying them in the first place?[15]

For both men, American slavery was the chief obstacle to maintaining unity. In the Revolutionary era, that obstacle was surmounted by constitutional compromises that still maintained a unity of political principles spelled out in the Declaration of Independence. Decades later, when the compromises with slavery led some Americans to demand that slavery be lawful throughout the nation, that unity was severely disrupted and threatened to split the nation permanently. That was the situation Lincoln faced when he bade farewell to his Springfield neighbors on February 11, 1861. This led him to conclude that he was heading to the nation's capital with a task before him "greater than that which rested upon Washington."

In his Springfield remarks, Lincoln also connected Washington to a watchful God, who seconded his efforts to unite the American colonies in their attempt to separate from Great Britain and govern themselves as an independent people. "Without the assistance of that Divine Being, who ever attended him," Lincoln reflected, "I cannot succeed. With that assistance I cannot fail." He went on to confess his reliance on God to be with him and the American people: "Trusting in Him, who can go with me, and remain with you and be every where for good, let us confidently hope that all will yet be well. To His care commending you, as I hope in your prayers you will commend me, I bid you an affectionate farewell."[16] He displayed a double piety or reverence as he extolled both the nation's founding father and the God to whom the founding fathers appealed in so many public documents. Lincoln's reliance on "that Divine Being, who ever attended him," became a regular appeal at moments when he also appealed to the support and efforts of the American people.

At his first inauguration, he stated, "If the Almighty Ruler of nations, with his eternal truth and justice, be on your side of the North, or on yours of the South, that truth, and that justice, will surely prevail, by the judgment of this great tribunal, the American people." After the war began, he called Congress into special session on July 4, 1861, and concluded his address by exhorting the nation to "renew our trust in God, and go forward without fear, and with manly hearts." In his first State of the Union address, Lincoln closed his speech with a similar overture to the Almighty and the American people: "With a reliance on Providence, all the more firm and earnest, let us proceed in the great task which events have devolved upon us." Throughout his life, Lincoln wrestled with the concept of human agency in light of the traditional notion of the sovereignty of God. With Washington setting precedent for the American citizenry to acknowledge their dependence on the providence of God, Lincoln followed suit with public statements that consistently linked public action with providential blessing.[17]

During the Civil War, Lincoln praised Washington on his birthday for his public acknowledgement of God's providence. "The birthday of Washington, and the Christian Sabbath, coinciding this year, and suggesting together, the highest interests of this life, and of that to come, is most propitious for the meeting proposed." Here Lincoln preached what Washington practiced, reliance on the Almighty for the success of the American experiment, extolling those who would "strengthen our reliance on the Supreme Being, for the final triumph of the right." A few months earlier, Lincoln had followed the example of Washington in issuing general orders intended to accommodate the Sabbath observance by members of the military: "The importance for man and beast of the prescribed weekly rest, the sacred rights of Christian soldiers and sailors, a becoming deference to the best sentiment of a Christian people, and a due regard for the Divine will, demand that Sunday labor in the Army and Navy be reduced to the measure of strict necessity." The order went on to quote General Washington's order verbatim: "The General hopes and trusts that every officer and man will endeavor to live and act as becomes a Christian soldier defending the dearest rights and liberties of his country." It also noted that Washington's order was the "first General Order issued by the Father of his Country after the Declaration of Independence," which "indicated the spirit in which our institutions were founded and should ever be defended." Lincoln appealed to Washington's Sabbath observance for the military as an example of accommodating the religious sentiments of the nation in a manner that allowed citizens to fulfill their religious duty while serving their country at its most trying hour.[18]

Lincoln continued to appeal to Washington as the quintessential moral leader of America throughout his public career. For example, in a speech before the Springfield Washington Temperance Society, Lincoln hailed Washington as "the mightiest name of earth—long since mightiest in the cause of civil liberty; still mightiest in moral reformation." He cited Washington as a past protector of civil liberty and—no doubt, recalling Weems's story of Washington and the cherry tree—as an abiding example in the cause of moral reform. "To add brightness to the sun, or glory to the name of Washington, is alike impossible," Lincoln said, closing the address by exhorting his audience: "Let none attempt it. In solemn awe pronounce the name, and in its naked deathless splendor, leave it shining on." Six years later, as a newly elected Whig congressman, Lincoln joined his rival, newly elected Democratic senator Stephen A. Douglas, to form the Illinois delegation on a committee preparing the celebration of Washington's birthday in the nation's capital. That year they would also represent their state at the National Birth-Right Ball held in Washington to support the building of the Washington Monument. Lincoln would continue to cite the name of Washington as an example of moral integrity and manly character.[19]

For example, during his one term in the House of Representatives, Lincoln scolded President James K. Polk for starting the Mexican-American War on false pretenses. He questioned the "spot" where Polk claimed Americans were killed by Mexican forces: "Let him remember he sits where Washington sat, and so remembering, let him answer, as Washington would answer."[20] Lincoln tried to shame Polk regarding how the Mexican-American War began by challenging him to measure his actions by the ethical standard set by Washington. In his 1783 Circular to the States, as Washington prepared to resign as commander in chief, he urged state governors to make sure the United States paid off the debts of the Revolutionary War: "Honesty will be found on every experiment, to be the best and only true policy."[21] Washington insisted that not only the nation's independence but also its honor and character were at stake. Similarly, Lincoln saw the war against Mexico as a question of morality, going so far as to cite the biblical Golden Rule in an 1848 letter to a Baptist preacher who had called the war "no aggression on Mexico." When considering the fate of the Mexicans, Lincoln asked, "is the precept 'Whatsoever ye would that men should do to you, do ye even so to them' obsolete?— of no force?—of no application?" Had it been "the humblest of our people" invaded by an army that ran roughshod over their crops, Lincoln doubted the preacher would consider the matter "too small for notice." Lincoln thought of the nation's war with Mexico in light of morality and national character, and in so doing, Washington represented his standard-bearer of national probity and honor.[22]

George Washington's character remained foremost in Lincoln's mind in the early months of the Civil War when he called forth state militias to put down the rebellion.[23] Federal troops at Fort Sumter in Charleston Harbor, South Carolina, had been compelled to sur-render and evacuate, and Lincoln was determined to shore up his defenses in preparation for further developments from Maryland and Virginia, both of which bordered Washington, D.C. For example, when a Massachusetts regiment and Pennsylvania volunteers tried to pass through Baltimore on their way to defend the nation's capital, a riot broke out in the secession-minded city.[24] Secretary of War Simon Cameron had called for regiments to be supplied by all states not claiming to have seceded from the Union. These included four regiments from Maryland, which were to assemble at Baltimore and Frederick City, Maryland.[25] When Baltimore citizens complained about the presence of federal troops, Lincoln called out their hypoc-risy regarding the hostile threat to the capital from Virginia: "You express great horror of bloodshed, and yet would not lay a straw in the way of those who are organizing in Virginia and elsewhere to capture this city." He then appealed to George Washington's char-acter to set them straight: "The rebels attack Fort Sumter, and your citizens attack troops sent to the defense of the Government, and the lives and property in Washington, and yet you would have me break my oath and surrender the Government without a blow. There is no Washington in that—no Jackson in that—no manhood nor honor in that." Lincoln refused to break his oath, the only one stipulated verbatim in the Constitution, which required the president to "pre-serve, protect, and defend the Constitution of the United States." Thus, Lincoln drew on Washington's courage and noble bearing as commander in chief during the Revolutionary War to shame his Baltimore visitors for complaining about federal actions taken to defend the nation's capital and government.[26]

In 1856, Lincoln promoted the presidential campaign of John C. Frémont, in part by associating the nascent Republican Party with the views of the founders. A pro-Frémont newspaper reported that Lincoln "demonstrated that the Republicans are walking in the 'old paths'—read the recorded sentiments of Washington, Jefferson and others, and dwelt at length upon the position of Henry Clay, (now quoted against him,) the Nestor of the old Whig party" and that he quoted "the declarations of these canonized leaders of both the great parties."[27] Lincoln included Thomas Jefferson, a standard-bearer of the Democratic Party, to bolster his nonpartisan appeal, and Henry Clay, who not only was a leader of the Whig Party but also was known for his efforts as "the Great Compromiser" to keep the American union together. In so doing, Lincoln attempted to fashion a public image of the new Republican Party as neither sectional nor radical. Instead, it promoted policies consistent with the principles and practices of the American founding.[28] Washington had long become synonymous with the noblest ideals and achievements of the American Revolution and thereby needed no elaboration or justification as part of an American pantheon of political saints emblematic of an older, trusted political order.

Lincoln continued this line of reasoning early in 1860 as the presidential campaigns took shape. In his February 1860 address at New York's Cooper Institute, which positioned Lincoln as a potential nominee of the Republican Party, he responded to those who "flaunt in our faces the warning against sectional parties given by Washington in his Farewell Address." They objected to the Republican Party's commitment to making the eventual abolition of slavery a national priority. Lincoln reminded them of Washington's earlier endorsement of the Northwest Ordinance of 1787, which prohibited slavery in the only territory the federal government owned at that time: "Washington . . . approved and signed an act of Congress, enforcing the prohibition of slavery in the North-western Territory, which act embodied the policy of the Government upon that subject up to and at the very moment he penned that warning." He cited Washington to rebut the charge that the Republican Party was sectional and therefore unworthy of consideration by an American people on the verge of civil war over the slavery controversy. Lincoln showed that Washington's warning about parties did not preclude him from speaking and acting to promote not just a unified but also a free nation, which meant the eventual abolition of slavery. The Northwest Ordinance (originally approved by the Articles of Confederation Congress on July 13, 1787), reauthorized by the first Congress under the Constitution framed in 1787, and signed by President George Washington on August 7, 1789, was just one step in the direction of an entirely free United States. "Could Washington himself speak," Lincoln added, "would he cast the blame of that sectionalism upon us, who sustain his policy, or upon you who repudiate it?" Lincoln affirmed that the Republican Party pledged nothing less than to follow Washington's example regarding freedom's ultimate triumph over slavery. Lincoln concluded that the unity Washington hoped for was a unity of moral purpose for the new republic—a nation that, despite the presence of slavery, would operate according to the principles of consent and the rule of law to secure the blessings of liberty, which required the eventual abolition of slavery.[29]

To complete his rebuttal of the sectionalism charge, Lincoln affirmed Washington's concern regarding it but added that it would apply more fittingly to those who would introduce a sectional defense of slavery's permanence in the United States: "We respect that warning of Washington, and we commend it to you, together with his example pointing to the right application of it." In Lincoln's mind, "the right application" of Washington's "warning against sectional parties" pertained to those who sought to strengthen slavery's hold on the American people—or those like Stephen Douglas, who espoused a policy of neutrality toward the spread of slavery—rather than those who sought to restrict its spread into the federal territories as a step toward its eventual elimination from all the American states. Slavery always was, and remained, the most divisive institution in the United States. Therefore, Lincoln and fellow Republicans promoted the gradual abolition of slavery as the most peaceful and unifying way of ridding the nation of the only institution that threatened to divide the American union.[30]

Lincoln concluded his Cooper Institute address by exhorting fellow Republicans not to give in to either proponents of popular sovereignty or defenders of slavery. Both political camps would make "Union appeals beseeching true Union men to yield to Disunionists, reversing the divine rule, and calling, not the sinners, but the righteous to repentance—such as invocations to Washington, imploring men to unsay what Washington said, and undo what Washington did."[31] In his 1858 senatorial debates with Lincoln, Democratic senator Stephen A. Douglas claimed the mantle of Washington and "the framers of this government" for his doctrine of popular sovereignty, "recognizing the right of each State to do as it pleased," which included whether to enslave black people. Douglas claimed to have drawn his policy of popular sovereignty from the leading statesmen of the Revolution, who respected the diversity of the American states and did not insist on making the new nation all free or all slave states: "Washington, Jefferson, Franklin, Madison, Hamilton, Jay, and the great men of that day, made this Government divided into free States and slave States, and left each State perfectly free to do as it pleased on the subject of slavery." In a January 1860 Senate speech intended to dash the presidential hopes of the Republican Party by tying it to the John Brown raid at Harpers Ferry, Douglas repeated the claim: "The framers of the Constitution knew . . . that our liberties depended upon reserving the right to the people of each State to make their own laws and establish their own institutions, and control them at pleasure, without interference from the Federal Government."[32] Lincoln rebutted these claims at Cooper Institute and, in doing so, drew national attention to his own potential as president.[33]

Lincoln drew again on Washington's reputation after the Civil War had begun and he had called Congress into special session to consider his actions in defense of the Union while it was out of session between March and July 1861. Near the end of his detailed speech, Lincoln praised the loyalty of the American people, for whom the Union represented a government "whose leading object is, to elevate the condition of men—to lift artificial weights from all shoulders—to clear the paths of laudable pursuit for all—to afford all, an unfettered start, and a fair chance, in the race of life." He lauded "the patriotic instinct of the plain people. They understand, without an argument, that destroying the government, which was made by Washington, means no good to them." By tying the common American to the founding American, Lincoln highlighted the efforts of soldiers and sailors who did not follow disloyal officers but "successfully resisted the traitorous efforts of those, whose commands, but an hour before, they obeyed as absolute law." Ironically enough, Lincoln fortified Washington's reputation as the American founder par excellence by connecting his disloyal actions toward England to the loyal actions of the plain men and women of America. Their "patriotic instinct" to defend the United States was a loyalty not simply to the only country they ever knew but also to one they understood was "made by Washington" not merely for his own benefit but for the benefit of all men.[34]

Lincoln acknowledged that "necessity" compelled Washington's generation to concede "to partial, and temporary departures" from pure republican principles when framing a better constitutional union than the Articles of Confederation and Perpetual Union. The slave interests of a few states insisted on some accommodations or they would not agree to a new constitution. Nevertheless, Washington understood these constitutional compromises to be exceptions to the rule established in the Declaration of Independence. Unlike "our good old one, signed by Washington," which began with "We the people," the constitution of the provisional Confederate States of America represented "the deputies of the sovereign and independent States." Lincoln asked, "Why this deliberate pressing out of view, the rights of men, and the authority of the people?" Equality and government by consent of the governed, as the founders understood them, found little room in the disloyal actions of citizens of the seceding states.[35]

"Our Fathers"

> We are striving to maintain the government and institutions
> of our fathers, to enjoy them ourselves, and transmit them to
> our children and our children's children forever.
>
> —Abraham Lincoln, Speech to the
> 148th Ohio Regiment (1864)

In addition to his appeal to *the* founding father, George Washington, Lincoln made frequent reference to "our fathers," the founding generation of statesmen who argued and fought for American independence. He used the terms *fathers*, *framers*, and *founders* interchangeably when lauding the ideals and governing structures of the generation that produced the Declaration of Independence and Constitution. Lincoln referred to the "founders" only a few times (and "Revolutionary patriarchs" once[36]), but his many references to the nation's political "fathers" and "framers" pointed to the generation that founded the American system of government on principles born of the struggle for independence.

The phrase "our fathers" has its origin in the Old Testament as a reference to the "fathers" of the Hebrew nation. Abraham, Isaac, and Jacob were the traditional "fathers" of the people of Israel. Their founding fathers, the leaders of the early generations of the Hebrew nation, were known as "our fathers." For example, Deuteronomy 26:3 says, "And thou shalt go unto the priest that shall be in those days, and say unto him, I profess this day unto the LORD thy God, that I am come unto the country which the LORD sware unto our fathers for to give us." The reference to "our fathers" was a familiar one for an American nation comprising a predominantly Christian population, whose pastors, preachers, and priests would have made ready reference to the Old Testament of the King James Bible, with its use of the phrase "our fathers," and to the New Testament, with the Lord's Prayer memorized by most churchgoers and beginning with "Our Father."

Whereas later generations of Hebrews were literal descendants of the fathers of Israel, only a small minority of Americans could claim a blood relation to the founding fathers of America. Lincoln observed that according to the founding fathers' claims in the Declaration of Independence, an American heritage derived not from blood but from a creed: "We hold these truths to be self-evident, that all men are created equal." Fatherhood according to a principle allowed subsequent generations of Americans to claim the founding fathers as their political fathers as long as they stayed devoted to the equality principle of the Declaration—"that moral sentiment taught in that day"—for "it is the father of all moral principle in them."[37] His use of "our fathers and grandfathers" aligned men of his generation with the American founders, demonstrating that the genius of America was something much deeper than blood ties to previous generations.

This religious use of "fathers" was a commonplace of politicians as well. Before Lincoln's inauguration as president, seven of his predecessors, as far back as Thomas Jefferson in his Second Inaugural

Address, referred to "fathers" or "forefathers" in their inaugural ad-dresses. Whereas Jefferson's reference to "our forefathers" was an appeal to the generation that crossed the Atlantic to America, the other presidents who cited the "fathers" or "forefathers" alluded to the leading men of the American Revolutionary era.[38] In his first formal debate with Lincoln in August 1858, Senator Stephen A. Douglas used "our fathers" to dispute Lincoln's claim about the founders' intentions for the future of slavery in America: "He tells you that it cannot endure permanently on the same principles and in the same relative condition in which our fathers made it. . . . Why can it not exist on the same principles on which our fathers made it?" He made this appeal to the nation's "fathers" again in subsequent debates that fall and repeatedly asserted a racial basis for the United States: "This government was made by our fathers on the white basis. It was made by white men for the benefit of white men and their posterity forever, and was intended to be administered by white men in all time to come."[39] Lincoln would make the proper interpretation of what the "fathers" believed a centerpiece of his 1858 campaign against Douglas for the U.S. Senate and when he spoke at Cooper Institute in a field test for his 1860 campaign for the presidency.

Both Lincoln and Douglas enlisted the nation's "fathers" in their debate about how to address the growing agitation over slavery. Douglas argued that the "fathers of the Revolution, and the sages who made the Constitution" saw that "a Republic as large as this, required different local and domestic regulations in each locality, adapted to the wants and interests of each separate State." The founding fathers established a federal Constitution that would allow states to "remain sovereign and supreme within their own limits in regard to all that was local, and internal, and domestic," including slavery. Douglas defended "the rights and sovereignty of the states" as the best way to preserve "diversity, dissimilarity, variety in all our local and domestic institutions." In sum, "the framers of our institutions were wise, saga-cious, and patriotic, when they . . . conferred upon each legislature the power to make all local and domestic institutions to suit the people it represented." He contrasted his respect for the diversity preserved by the fathers with what he called Lincoln's "doctrine of uniformity," which would impose "one consolidated empire" to impose equality throughout the diverse expanse of American states. After calling uniformity "the parent of despotism the world over," he applied this reasoning to the controversy over American slavery: "Wherever the doctrine of uniformity is proclaimed, that all the States must be free or all slave, that all labor must be white or all black, . . . you have destroyed the greatest safeguard which our institutions have thrown around the rights of the citizen." Douglas concluded that Lincoln "totally misapprehended the great principles upon which our government rests," which he attributed to misunderstanding what "the framers of the Constitution" devised to maintain both the diversity and unity of the American states.[40]

Douglas also cited the founding fathers to support his deference to the 1857 *Dred Scott* opinion, which Lincoln and fellow Republicans excoriated for its ruling that Congress did not have authority to ban slavery in the federal territories. "I am a law-abiding man," Douglas proclaimed, and "will sustain the Constitution of my country as our fathers have made it." By "Constitution," he meant Chief Justice Roger B. Taney's interpretation of it. Taney claimed the Fifth Amendment guaranteed a federal right to own slaves: "Thus, the rights of property are united with the rights of person, and placed on the same ground by the fifth amendment to the Constitution, which provides that no person shall be deprived of life, liberty, and property, without due process of law." According to Taney, "The right of property in a slave is distinctly and expressly affirmed in the Constitution." Not only could Congress not ban slavery in federal territory, as it did in the 1820 Missouri Compromise, but it possessed "the power coupled with the duty of guarding and protecting the owner in his rights." Douglas condemned Lincoln's disagreement with the *Dred Scott* opinion, which he viewed as "resisting the decision of the Supreme Court," and hoped that Lincoln and the Republican Party would be seen as lawless and subversive in their efforts to have Congress continue to ban slavery in federal territory despite the court's decision.[41]

Lincoln responded to Douglas the very next day, countering Douglas with his own references to the founders. He cited acts of Congress under the Articles of Confederation and the subsequent U.S. Constitution that restricted the importation of slaves and their introduction into the Northwest Territory. "What were they," Lincoln concluded, "but a clear indication that the framers of the Constitution intended and expected the ultimate extinction of that institution." He argued that "the founders of this Government originally placed it" on a gradual path to extinction, which kept the peace among the union of American states. A week later, he declared, "I wish to see slavery placed in the course of ultimate extinction—placed where our fathers originally placed it."[42]

In their formal debates later that summer and fall of 1858, Lincoln insisted that "the fathers" intended the eventual abolition of slavery. He campaigned against Douglas in hopes that slavery "should be placed back again upon the basis that the fathers of our government originally placed it upon." Lincoln believed slavery would "become extinct, for all time to come, if we but re-adopted the policy of the fathers by restricting it to the limits it has already covered—restricting it from the new Territories." Douglas had charged that by seeking the eventual elimination of slavery throughout the United States, Lincoln would provoke "a war of sections, a war of the North against the South, of the free states against the slave states." Lincoln replied that only by treating slavery as something wrong, at minimum "restricting the spread of it," could the nation eventually get rid of the only thing that "ever threatened the existence of this Union." He thought Douglas was absurd to promote a policy of popular sovereignty that required neutrality by the federal government toward slavery. For "if it is a wrong, he cannot say people have a right to do wrong." By limiting the spread of slavery and not attacking it directly where it already existed in certain states, Lincoln thought the founders had found a way to promote slavery's eventual eradication while maintaining the American union. "That is the peaceful way," Lincoln observed, "the old-fashioned way, the way in which the fathers themselves set us the example."[43]

Stephen Douglas retained his Senate seat in January 1859, but in the months leading up to the 1860 presidential election, Lincoln maintained that the founding fathers understood slavery to be a necessary evil that was to be treated as such where permitted under the federal Constitution. The early American republic was a time "in which our fathers adopted, and during which they followed a policy restricting the spread of slavery, and the whole Union was acquiescing in it." Lincoln concluded this point with emphasis: *As those fathers marked it, so let it be again marked, as an evil not to be extended, but to be tolerated and protected only because of and so far as its actual presence among us makes that toleration and protection a necessity.* Slavery existed before the Constitution was established, and colonial attempts to prevent continued slave importation were thwarted by King George III. Therefore, the founders chose to compromise with slavery where it then existed in order to establish and preserve the union of the American states.[44]

Lincoln made his most famous reference to "our fathers" in the fittingly archaic opening sentence of his Gettysburg Address: "Four score and seven years ago our fathers brought forth on this continent, a new nation, conceived in Liberty, and dedicated to the proposition that all men are created equal." Lincoln employed birth imagery— "brought forth," "conceived," and "dedicated"—to connect the pious reference of "our fathers" to the founders of "a new nation." The nation was new not simply because of the independence of the American people from England but, most important, because of the kind of nation they set out to establish: one where "Liberty" was both its means and its end. What the fathers of America brought into being was a country devoted to protecting the freedom of every American. Following the Declaration of Independence, Lincoln presented this freedom as the gift of God to every human being. With human equality as the bedrock foundation of America, the fathers set the young nation on a course to proving self-government was a legitimate and viable form of rule.[45]

That new nation proved unable to follow through on the founders' commitment to equality when citizens of eleven slaveholding states rejected the fathers' "proposition" and turned to war to establish the Confederate States of America. During that civil war, Lincoln eventually turned to emancipation as "a fit and necessary war measure" to help preserve a nation "so conceived and so dedicated."[46] The war produced a "new birth of freedom," but it did not supplant the original freedom conceived by the fathers. Instead of seeking new rights for a new age, Lincoln wanted loyal Americans to recommit themselves to the promise of the original plan of "our fathers"—to establish a nation where all men *created* equal would be *protected* equally. Richard Brookhiser writes of Lincoln's Gettysburg pledge, "If he had intended to write a blank check at Gettysburg, he would have called for 'a birth of new freedom' (or 'a birth of new freedoms'). What he did call for was 'a new birth of freedom.' His freedom was the old freedom, the freedom of 'our fathers.'"[47] Now "government of the people, by the people, for the people" on American soil would include freed slaves. With a victory over rebellious Americans, due in part to an emancipation that drew close to two hundred thousand black men into the Union army and navy, "a new birth of freedom" would entail the protection of all Americans, which included 3 to 4 million freedmen at the war's end and the ratification of the Thirteenth Amendment.

A year later, Lincoln repeated this interpretation of the meaning of the Civil War when he contrasted the founding fathers with an even older, earlier set of fathers—the Pilgrims. Lincoln turned down an invitation to attend a festival in New York commemorating the landing of the Pilgrims but congratulated the organizers for their devotion to the Union cause. Affirming the Pilgrim effort as "the glory of their age" and deserving due respect, Lincoln maintained, "How vastly greater is our opportunity" to "complete and perpetuate the work our fathers began and transmitted." He invited them to honor the memory of the Pilgrims but to take heart from the example of more recent and more momentous fathers, the fathers of the American republic, to meet their own generation's challenge. That opportunity was to vindicate the viability of self-government by defending it against internal enemies. While all regimes, democratic and otherwise, are subject to external threats, democracies had yet to demonstrate that they were capable of perpetuating themselves in the face of internal disruption. Ancient republics had lost their liberty through an inability to live within the constraints they imposed on themselves. Lincoln praised the "devoted unanimity" of civilian and servicemen in their resolution not to allow the rebellion to succeed—a rebellion begun by a refusal to abide by the constitutional election of a man with whom they disagreed politically.[48]

Lincoln viewed the Union cause as a defense of human liberty and equality against the retrograde principles of human slavery and caste. In that sense, defenders of the American union were advancing the progress of the human condition and thereby giving the world hope that America's example could be replicated elsewhere and ultimately everywhere. Lincoln's appeal to Washington and "the fathers" was intended to help his generation appreciate what was founded and how that founding could ultimately secure liberty for all. The next chapter, with its focus on the Declaration of Independence, illustrates most clearly what Lincoln understood were the founders' aims in establishing an independent nation.

LINCOLN AND THE DECLARATION
OF INDEPENDENCE: AN APPEAL
TO THE FOUNDERS' ENDS

I have never had a feeling politically that did not spring from
the sentiments embodied in the Declaration of Independence.
—Abraham Lincoln, Address in Independence
Hall, Philadelphia (1861)

As much as Lincoln held George Washington in high esteem for
his leadership in founding the United States, he drew most of
his guidance not from a founding person but from a founding document—the Declaration of Independence. The Declaration is the sine
qua non of Lincoln's political thought. It was the most influential
source from the founding era that he cited to equip Americans to
deal with the agitation over slavery and the growing sectional crisis
of the 1850s.

During his 1858 campaign against Stephen Douglas for the U.S.
Senate, Lincoln harked back to what he called "that old Declaration
of Independence" to show that the origin of popular sovereignty
rightly understood was not new but dated to the American founding.
Speaking a week after the Fourth of July celebrations, he argued that
the principles of human equality and government by consent of the
governed were established long before Douglas came on the political
scene. Lincoln called the framers of the Constitution "those old men"

when referring to the Northwest Ordinance of 1787, which included a ban on slavery in the only territory owned by the federal government at that time. He looked to an old document and "old men" for guidance in addressing a new situation: putting slavery back on the "course of ultimate extinction," where Lincoln thought "the founders of this Government originally placed it." He believed that the nation's prosperity had everything to do with its original commitment to equality, observing that "our fathers and grandfathers . . . were iron men, they fought for the principle that they were contending for; and we understood that by what they then did it has followed that the degree of prosperity that we now enjoy has come to us."[1]

But then he pointed out that the United States was also populated by men who, "finding themselves our equals in all things," cannot trace their heritage to the founding generation by blood. Nevertheless, when they read the Declaration of Independence and saw the principle of human equality, they rightly felt a kinship to the founders. Moreover, they believed that the equality concept was "the father of all moral principle in them, and that they have a right to claim it as though they were blood of the blood, and flesh of the flesh of the men who wrote that Declaration, and so they are." With a right understanding of their past, and by staying true to that past, Lincoln believed even those of his generation who could not trace their family lineage to actual American ancestors could still call themselves descendants of the men who wrote the Declaration. He likened the association made by immigrants (or children of immigrants) to the founding generation to Adam beholding Eve for the first time: "This is now bone of my bones, and flesh of my flesh: she shall be called Woman, because she was taken out of Man" (Gen. 2:23).[2] The principle of human equality made possible a political kinship freed from the Old World tradition of blood and soil. Lincoln called the equality principle "the electric cord in that Declaration that links the hearts of patriotic and liberty-loving men together, that will link those patriotic hearts as long as the love of freedom exists in the minds of men throughout the world." He believed that to interpret the Declaration as favoring a particular race or nationality would "rub out the sentiment of liberty in the country" and "transform this government into a government of some other form." This would be no different than "the arguments that kings have made for enslaving the people in all ages of the world" and therefore no improvement on the arbitrary ways of the Old World.[3]

A few months after Lincoln fell short in his campaign to replace Douglas in the U.S. Senate, he was invited to give a speech in Boston to commemorate the birthday of the author of the Declaration of Independence, Thomas Jefferson. A local commitment prevented him from attending, but Lincoln sent a testimonial to Jefferson to be read in his absence. It was subsequently published in Republican newspapers in at least five states.[4] In it he declared that the "principles of Jefferson are the definitions and axioms of free society." To speak of "definitions and axioms" is to speak the language of Euclidean geometry, which begins with definitions, postulates, and "common notions," also known as axioms. Lincoln actually noted in an 1860 campaign autobiography that he "studied and nearly mastered the Six-books of Euclid, since he was a member of Congress." Just as Euclid's definitions and axioms are the first principles of geometry, Lincoln understood the principles of Jefferson—meaning the self-evident truths of the Declaration—to be the building blocks of free government. In 1859, with the Democratic Party becoming the national defender of slavery, Lincoln saw an opportunity to claim the mantle of Jefferson and the principles of the Declaration of Independence for the Republican Party.[5]

"All honor to Jefferson," Lincoln declared, "to the man who, in the concrete pressure of a struggle for national independence by a single people, had the coolness, forecast, and capacity to introduce into a merely revolutionary document, an abstract truth, applicable to all men and all times." The Declaration was not just an announcement of the American colonists' decision to rule themselves. Its statement of political principle applied to any people, any time and anywhere, who had not consented to their form of government and were not secure in the exercise of their natural rights. Lincoln praised Jefferson for basing American independence on a standard by which their own future conduct could be judged. In this fashion, a timeless "abstract truth" could play a practical role by serving as "a rebuke and a stumbling-block to the very harbingers of re-appearing tyranny and oppression." Lincoln read the Declaration as a founding rebuke of Stephen Douglas and the Democratic Party insofar as their principles departed from those of the author of the Declaration of Independence.[6]

Considering that Thomas Jefferson was a Democrat and Lincoln was a Whig, and later a Republican, one might be surprised to learn of Lincoln's effusive praise of Jefferson. Given their partisan differences, Lincoln was said to have held Jefferson in low regard as a politician. In 1870, his most assiduous contemporary biographer and junior law partner, William Herndon, wrote, "Mr. Lincoln hated Thomas Jefferson as a man—rather as a politician." However, when asked during the fall campaign for the presidency in 1860, Lincoln denied saying "anything derogatory of Mr. Jefferson" and said a newspaper article attributed to him that disparaged Jefferson was "a base forgery." When commenting on Jefferson through speeches or letters intended for a public audience, Lincoln was all praise for the author of the Declaration of Independence.[7]

Lincoln once lauded Jefferson as "the most distinguished politician of our history" and the originator of "the policy of prohibiting slavery in new territory." By this he meant Jefferson's original proposal that the Articles of Confederation Congress ban slavery from the Northwest Territory, which included a vast land tract ceded by the Commonwealth of Virginia. His 1784 draft resolution stipulated that "after the year 1800 of the Christian era, there shall be neither slavery nor involuntary servitude in any of the said states" arising from that territory. That Congress eventually passed a revised version of Jefferson's proposal, the Northwest Ordinance of 1787. Therefore, "away back of the constitution," Lincoln noted, "in the pure fresh, free breath of the revolution, the State of Virginia, and the National congress put that policy in practice." During his 1858 debates with Douglas, he cited Jefferson's proposal to prevent slavery's expansion into federal territory to argue that Congress should not allow slavery to expand by sacrificing moral right to mere commercial interests: "There is no reason in favor of sending slavery to Kansas that might not be adduced in support of the African slave trade. Each are demanded by the profitableness of the traffic thus made in opening a new slave mart, and not from the rightfulness of it." If Congress permitted slavery to enter a federal territory, Lincoln thought it would not be long before Congress removed the ban against the importation of slaves into states. Rejecting an interpretation of equality in the Declaration that Stephen Douglas applied only to "British white subjects," Lincoln asked, "Are Jeffersonian Democrats willing to have the gem taken from the magna charta of human liberty in this shameful way? Or will they maintain that its declaration of equality of natural rights among all nations is correct?" Lincoln traced the policy of nonextension of slavery into territories, the future states of the Union, back to Thomas Jefferson. He may have been a Democratic icon, but more important, he was the author of the Declaration of Independence.[8]

Lincoln did not mention Jefferson's later opinion that emancipation would come for American slaves sooner and peacefully if slavery were actually permitted to expand into the western territories. During the 1820 controversy over Missouri entering the Union as a slave state, Jefferson recommended "a general emancipation and *expatriation*" as the most prudent course of action over the long term. Their "diffusion" over the country would dilute the black slave population vis-à-vis the white population, making emancipation more likely if white masters no longer feared reprisal.[9] Lincoln never endorsed this later view of Jefferson's, convinced that wherever slavery planted itself, it became all the more difficult to uproot. For example, after the passage of the Kansas-Nebraska Act would allow slavery to enter through local popular sovereignty, Lincoln lamented that "opening of new countries to slavery, tends to the perpetuation of the institution, and so does KEEP men in slavery who otherwise would be free." Better to prevent its introduction than to attempt its removal once established. While Lincoln agreed with Jefferson that emancipation would have to happen gradually in order to happen peacefully, he believed a congressional ban on slavery in the federal territories was necessary to put slavery on the path to ultimate extinction.[10]

Lincoln's reverence for the Declaration of Independence made him a student of John Locke even though he had never read the quintessential source of Enlightenment political theory, Locke's *Second Treatise of Civil Government*.[11] In a 1789 letter, Jefferson cited Locke along with Isaac Newton and Francis Bacon as "the three greatest men that have ever lived, without any exception, and as having laid the foundation of those superstructures which have been raised in the Physical and Moral sciences." In an 1825 letter, Jefferson mentioned Locke as a key influence in the drafting of the Declaration of Independence. Describing the Declaration as "an expression of the American mind," he explained that "its authority rests then on the harmonizing sentiments of the day, whether expressed in conversation, in letters, printed essays, or in the elementary books of public right, as Aristotle, Cicero, Locke, Sidney, &c."[12] Despite the lack of evidence that Lincoln ever read John Locke, his frequent references to the Declaration of Independence and other writings of Jefferson reflected several key principles of Locke's political philosophy.[13]

En route to his inauguration as president, Lincoln spoke at Independence Hall, where the Second Continental Congress met during the Revolutionary War. He stated, "All the political sentiments I entertain have been drawn . . . from the sentiments which originated, and were given to the world from this hall." The representatives of the American colonies meeting in Philadelphia deliberated over the next step to take regarding the growing conflict with England. Already a year into the war for American independence, the Second Continental Congress approved a resolution by Virginia delegate Richard Henry Lee on July 2, 1776, which declared, "That these United Colonies are, and of right ought to be, free and independent States, that they are absolved from all allegiance to the British Crown, and that all political connection between them and the State of Great Britain is, and ought to be, totally dissolved." Two days later, the more famous Declaration of Independence was approved, justifying the bold course of action taken by the American colonists.[14]

Mindful that citizens of seven slaveholding states had issued ordinances of secession in the few months following his November election, Lincoln thought out loud in his Philadelphia remarks about "what great principle or idea it was that kept this Confederacy so long together." With division over the meaning of the federal

Constitution, especially in regard to the protection it owed to slavery in the territories following the infamous *Dred Scott v. Sanford* decision, Lincoln drew the nation's attention to the Declaration of Independence to find what was once a source of unity for Americans. He observed that independence, while the obvious end to which the American colonists had pledged "our Lives, our Fortunes, and our sacred Honor," was not an end in itself. More than "the mere matter of the separation of the colonies from the mother land," Lincoln argued, the Declaration gave "liberty, not alone to the people of this country, but hope to the world for all future time." He claimed that the liberty for which Americans were then willing to die was not theirs alone to possess but the birthright of all human beings. The implication was that even the enslaved Africans on American soil deserved their freedom.[15]

Of course, Lincoln was aware that slavery was not immediately abolished during the American Revolution. He stated that the Declaration "gave promise that in due time the weights should be lifted from the shoulders of all men, and that *all* should have an equal chance." The security of one's natural rights would come "in due time." War, ignorance, selfishness, habit, survival, and so many other obstacles and contingencies posed hindrances to the fulfillment of the Declaration's promise, for all Americans as well as the rest of the world. However, Lincoln believed that the American founders did not replace one set of oppressors with another. As he noted in 1857, Stephen Douglas's interpretation of the Declaration of Independence "gave no promise that having kicked off the King and Lords of Great Britain, we should not at once be saddled with a King and Lords of our own." Contrary to Douglas, Lincoln understood the struggle for independence as based on the equality of all human beings.[16]

Lincoln declared that equal liberty was the true aim of the American Revolution, and he asked, "Now, my friends, can this country be saved upon that basis?" He invited Americans to return to an older understanding of the Declaration and hence an older interpretation of the Constitution, a document also drafted in Independence Hall. Ten days away from his presidential inauguration, and with the lower South preparing for war, Lincoln insisted, "There is no need of bloodshed and war" and "there will be no blood shed unless it be forced upon the Government." A war of self-defense, with Lincoln as commander in chief, would be worth the cost only if America were preserved for the sake of the liberty described in the Declaration. "But, if this country cannot be saved without giving up that principle," he confessed, "I would rather be assassinated on this spot than to surrender it." This was no exaggerated boast, as Lincoln had been warned the night before his Independence Hall speech of an assassination plot to take place in Baltimore. He would arrive in Washington, D.C., secretly the day after his travel through Pennsylvania.[17] The principle of human equality, along with several others directly stated or implied in the Declaration of Independence, would constitute the basis of Lincoln's political thought.

Human Equality

> We understand that the "equality of man" principle which actuated our forefathers in the establishment of the government is right; and that slavery, being directly opposed to this, is morally wrong.
>
> —Abraham Lincoln, Speech at
> Hartford, Connecticut (1860)

The most famous statement of the Declaration of Independence is "that all men are created equal." Lincoln's understanding of this equality was the traditional understanding articulated by John Locke and other philosophers of the Enlightenment. Locke posited that the natural state of human beings, antecedent to the formation of government, was an "equality" of authority over themselves and their possessions: "wherein all the power and jurisdiction is reciprocal, no one having more than another; . . . equal one amongst another without subordination or subjection." He added that this natural state was "a state of perfect freedom to order their actions, and dispose of their possessions and persons, as they think fit, within the bounds of the law of nature, without asking leave, or depending upon the will of any other man."[18] For Locke, to derive the principles of just government correctly, one needed to know the natural status of human beings: first articulate what a human being is, then one can determine the purpose and powers of government.

Lincoln's concise formulation of self-government was that "each man should do precisely as he pleases with all which is exclusively his own." He said this "lies at the foundation of the sense of justice there is in me." Lincoln referred to Locke's concept of a state of nature when he argued that Henry Clay's reading of the Declaration included black people in principle: "If a state of nature existed and we were about to lay the foundations of society, *no man would be more strongly opposed than I should be, to incorporating the institution of slavery among its elements.*" In a letter three days later, he repeated Clay's reference to a Lockean state of nature: "In our new free teritories, a state of nature *does* exist. In them Congress lays the foundations of society; and, in laying those foundations, I say, with Mr. Clay, it is desireable that the declaration of the equality of all men shall be kept in view, as a great fundamental principle." Lincoln agreed with Clay that in regulating federal territory, Congress, "which lays the foundations of society, should . . . be strongly opposed to the incorporation of slavery." If all men were created equal, then slavery should not be introduced into a territory where it did not already exist.[19]

In 1854, Lincoln cited the practice of white Southerners who had freed their slaves to show they did not really believe that black people were simply brute creatures like farm animals. At a fundamental level, they believed they were equally human: "And now, why will you ask us to deny the humanity of the slave? and estimate him only as the equal of the hog?" Lincoln pointed out how more than four hundred thousand free black people resided in the District of Columbia and other federal territories "without owners." That would never happen with horses or cattle. Those black people had been slaves themselves, or were descendants of slaves, but "at vast pecuniary sacrifices" were freed by their white owners. Why? "In all these cases," Lincoln observed, "it is your sense of justice, and human sympathy, continually telling you, that the poor negro has some natural right to himself—that those who deny it, and make mere merchandise of him, deserve kickings, contempt and death."[20]

His reference to death may sound exaggerated, but in 1820, Congress equated the importation of slaves into the United States with piracy, which carried the punishment of death. This statute reinforced the original law passed on March 2, 1807 and signed by President Thomas Jefferson to take effect on January 1, 1808, the earliest that Congress could ban the importation of slaves under the U.S. Constitution. Article I, Section 9, reads, "The Migration or Importation of such Persons as any of the States now existing shall think proper to admit shall not be prohibited by the Congress prior to the Year one thousand eight hundred and eight." As Lincoln liked to point out, the framers studiously avoided using the word *slave* in the Constitution, always referring to "person" or "persons" in the few clauses dealing with slavery.[21]

Lincoln used the fact of Southern manumission to shore up the conscience of white Southerners and show why slavery should not be allowed where it had not yet entered—for example, in the Kansas and Nebraska Territories, where Stephen Douglas applied popular sovereignty. Given that Congress could not free slaves in the states where they already existed, Lincoln knew that abolition would occur there only if the citizens of those states saw fit to do so. Therefore, he did what he could rhetorically to encourage them along those lines. Unlike the abolitionists, Lincoln did not publicly condemn white Southerners for their long-standing practice of enslaving fellow human beings but pointed out the ways they had acted in the most humane and civilized fashion in emancipating slaves here and there, over time, and at great personal cost.[22]

He then refuted Douglas's popular sovereignty, which Douglas had called "that great principle of self-government." Douglas's Kansas-Nebraska Act of 1854 repealed the Missouri Compromise of 1820 by allowing local settlers of the Kansas and Nebraska Territories to determine for themselves whether they would permit slavery—something explicitly barred by the terms of the Missouri Compromise in territory located above the 36°30' parallel. Douglas interpreted popular sovereignty as permitting rule by the white majority over the black minority, which meant black people would only exercise privileges deemed by the majority white population as consistent with their safety and comfort.[23]

Lincoln affirmed self-government as "absolutely and eternally right" but did not believe Douglas understood the concept correctly because he did not apply it to black people. Lincoln countered that "if the negro *is* a man, is it not to that extent, a total destruction of self-government, to say that he too shall not govern *himself*?" According to Lincoln's interpretation of the Declaration, the premise of self-government was human equality, not race, color, or some other arbitrary characteristic. He argued that to treat people differently because of race was no different from tyranny: "When the white man governs himself that is self-government; but when he governs himself, and also governs *another* man, that is more than self-government—that is despotism." He concluded, "If the negro is a man, why then my ancient faith teaches me that 'all men are created equal'; and that there can be no moral right in connection with one man's making a slave of another." He distinguished moral right from legal right because of the compromise with slavery that was necessary to keep the union of American states together at the time of the founding. But Lincoln argued that the way to move from slavery to emancipation was to remind white Americans of the equal humanity of black slaves and therefore of the moral obligation to abolish slavery as soon as practicable.[24]

In contrast with human equality, which formed the basis of genuine self-government, Douglas's version of popular sovereignty was simply rule by the arbitrary, numerical might of white people over so-called inferior races. Lincoln thought that government by mere majority will misconstrued the founders' understanding of self-government. He worried that by degrees, Americans were "giving up the OLD for the NEW faith." The American people once declared that all men were created equal, but Lincoln now lamented, "from that beginning we have run down to the other declaration, that for SOME men to enslave OTHERS is a 'sacred right of self-government.' These principles can not stand together. They are as opposite as God and mammon; and whoever holds to the one, must despise the other." Lincoln's comparison of human equality and popular sovereignty to God and mammon alluded to Matthew 6:24: "No man can serve two masters: for either he will hate the one, and love the other; or else he will hold to the one, and despise the other. Ye cannot serve God and mammon." With mammon representing the greed and wealth that drove the slave industry, tempting white people to enslave black people if there was money to be made, Lincoln contrasted the equality principle of the Declaration with the popular sovereignty policy of the Kansas-Nebraska Act. He concluded, "The spirit of seventy-six and the spirit of Nebraska, are utter antagonisms," and warned, "The former is being rapidly displaced by the latter." By distinguishing "the first precept of our ancient faith" from the supposedly "'sacred right' of taking slaves to Nebraska," Lincoln hoped to demonstrate the incompatibility of Douglas's counterfeit popular sovereignty with the Declaration's human equality.[25]

He concluded his comparison of the spirit of seventy-six with the spirit of Nebraska with a magisterial ode to the founding principle enshrined in the Declaration of Independence: "Our republican robe is soiled, and trailed in the dust. Let us repurify it. Let us turn and wash it white, in the spirit, if not the blood, of the Revolution. Let us turn slavery from its claims of 'moral right,' back upon its existing legal rights, and its arguments of 'necessity.'" He exhorted his audience to return slavery "to the position our fathers gave it; and there let it rest in peace." Lincoln employed a pun, "rest in peace" (or *requiescat in pace*, the gravestone RIP), to suggest that the peace established by the founders was twofold: first, it was the immediate peace facilitated by the compromise over slavery, which enabled the diverse American colonies to unite as one independent nation; second, it alluded to the ultimate peace of the grave that the founders intended for slavery once the new American republic established itself. The founding fathers considered slavery a necessary evil, but as Lincoln understood it, they believed they were morally obligated to kill it as soon as practicable for the United States to be a truly self-governing country.[26]

Lincoln's imagery of a soiled robe portrayed the free nation's need for renewal, if not redemption. In the Book of Revelation, God grants a vision of the saved to John the Apostle: "And he said unto me, These are they which came out of great tribulation, and have washed their long robes, and have made their long robes white in the blood of the Lamb" (Rev. 7:14). Lincoln depicted an America saved by the spirit of the American Revolution, the spirit of '76. It was a spirit born of the founding era's sacrifice of blood and treasure to establish a country devoted to human equality even as it struggled to wrest itself from the clutches of slavery. Moved by the spirit of the founding, Lincoln urged fellow Americans to "re-adopt the Declaration of Independence, and with it, the practices, and policy, which harmonize with it." Most important, Americans "north and south, . . . all lovers of liberty everywhere," needed to treat slavery as an evil to be tolerated in the short run because of constitutional obligation and eliminated in the long run because of moral obligation. In so doing, they would "join in the great and good work" begun by the founders.[27]

If Americans returned to the path set out by the founders, Lincoln declared, "we shall not only have saved the Union; but we shall have so saved it, as to make, and to keep it, forever worthy of the saving." A return to the founders' ideal that all men are created equal would save an America that would light the way for people across the globe to do the same. "We shall have so saved it," Lincoln proclaimed, "that the succeeding millions of free happy people, the world over, shall rise up, and call us blessed, to the latest generations." Only by remembering the founding principle of human equality and therefore aspiring to have the government protect its citizens equally, regardless of color or any other arbitrary characteristic, would the United States of America be "forever worthy of the saving" and continue to stand as a beacon of hope for humanity the world over.[28]

This equal humanity, what the Declaration described as the endowment of the Creator of all human beings, is typically referred to today as individual dignity. Christian theologians call it the *imago dei*, the idea that all people are made in the image of God. As Genesis 1:26–27 states, "And God said, Let us make man in our image, after our likeness . . . So God created man in his own image, in the image of God created he him; male and female created he them." Lincoln drew his Lockean understanding of human equality not only from the Declaration of Independence but also from the Bible.

Early in his 1858 campaign against Stephen Douglas, Lincoln inter-preted the Declaration as a proclamation of the founders' "sacred principles" of humanity to "the whole world of men." Almost all the original American states represented "slaveholding communities," but their efforts to abolish the slave trade marked the beginning of the gradual elimination of slavery. This was a clear sign to Lincoln that they "greatly deplored the evil," especially as it contradicted the self-evident truth "that all men are created equal." That equality statement, in Lincoln's words, reflected "their majestic interpretation of the economy of the Universe. This was their lofty, and wise, and noble understanding of the justice of the Creator to His creatures. Yes, gentlemen, to all His creatures, to the whole great family of man." He continued, "In their enlightened belief, nothing stamped with the Divine image and likeness was sent into the world to be trod-den on, and degraded, and imbruted by its fellows." When Lincoln postponed a death sentence for the crime of slave importation, he referred to the fatherhood of God to all those created in His image: "In granting this respite, it becomes my painful duty to admonish the prisoner that, relinquishing all expectation of pardon by Hu-man Authority, he refer himself alone to the mercy of the common God and Father of all men." Lincoln took the occasion of a pending execution to remind Nathaniel Gordon, the convicted slave trader, of the enormity of his crime: it was unlawful not only in the eyes of his political community but also according to the God who had made him as well as the men, women, and children he treated as mere merchandise. It would become the only time an American president hanged a person for importing slaves. However, by rejecting Gordon's petition to commute his sentence to life imprisonment, and allow-ing the prisoner a couple of weeks to prepare himself for "the awful change which awaits him," Lincoln signaled how wrong it was to turn one's fellow human beings into articles of commerce.[29]

In no speech did Lincoln make equality more central to American self-government than in his remarks at the dedication of the nation's first national cemetery in Gettysburg, Pennsylvania. "Four score and seven years ago our fathers brought forth on this continent, a new nation, conceived in Liberty, and dedicated to the proposition that all men are created equal." The most famous opening of the most famous speech in American history dates the nation's birth not to the framing of the Constitution but to the Declaration of Independence. More important than their governing structures was their governing purpose: to protect human equality. In the midst of a civil war produced by rival interpretations of what the Constitution required regarding slavery, Lincoln directed the nation's attention back to its founding charter and its claim about human equality. Whereas his First Inaugural Address did not focus on the Declaration of Independence or the principle of human equality, his Gettysburg Address harked back to the equal rights of humanity as the central motive of the American regime. After the repulse of General Robert E. Lee at Gettysburg, Lincoln wanted Americans to "dedicate" themselves to the task that remained: to honor those who fought at Gettysburg on behalf of the Union by supporting their cause and bringing it to fruition. It was a fight to bring forth a truly free political community: "government of the people, by the people, for the people."[30]

Lincoln delivered the Gettysburg Address in the Year of Jubilee, the year of his Emancipation Proclamation. On January 1, 1863, the president had charged Union soldiers and sailors to protect the freedom of over 3 million black people formerly enslaved in rebel-held territory. What Lincoln called "a new birth of freedom" was tied directly to the old, original birth of freedom, a freedom that naturally belonged to all human beings. He did not announce a new principle of freedom but affirmed an old claim: that liberty was the equal possession of every human being. Lincoln spoke not of a new work, but of "the unfinished work" to which the living could dedicate themselves. In this way, they could honor the loyal men at Gettysburg "who gave their lives that that nation might live."[31]

Having emancipated most of the slaves in the Union, Lincoln asked his countrymen to finish a war whose beneficiaries would now include millions of black freedmen. White Americans would now have to see that saving the American Union, and therewith "government of the people, by the people, for the people," entailed saving a Constitution for black people as well as white people. Lincoln's wartime efforts to inform public opinion would achieve their greatest victory if white people were persuaded to accept black people as equal members of the American social and political order. Before the war, he argued that the "central idea" of American public opinion "at the beginning was, and until recently has continued to be, 'the equality of men.'"[32] Immediately after the war, Lincoln's absence from the political landscape failed to produce a statesman who could restore human equality as the driver of national public policy.

Individual Rights

> I believe each individual is naturally entitled to do as he pleases with himself and the fruit of his labor, so far as it in no wise interferes with any other man's rights.
> —Abraham Lincoln, Speech at Chicago (1858)

To say that "all men are created equal" invites the question, "Equal in what way?" The Declaration elaborates on the equality of all people by affirming "that they are endowed by their Creator with certain inalienable rights, that among these are life, liberty, and the pursuit of happiness." More than a general notion of humanity or individual dignity, human equality entailed something more specific: the equal possession of rights or liberties. Lincoln believed that all human beings were born with rights, which were not the gift or creation of human societies or government. The chief task of government, therefore, was not to give but to protect rights—to make it safe for individuals to exercise their rights. As the Declaration states, "That to secure these rights, governments are instituted among men." How does one understand the equal rights possessed by all human beings but protected unequally by a founding generation that explicitly declared human equality as the basis of separating from England? It was precisely this question that Lincoln answered in the critical years preceding the Civil War as he sought to preserve the American Union from ideas and policies that undermined the conviction that all men are created equal.

Lincoln's speech criticizing the 1857 *Dred Scott* opinion is the best explication of the principles of the Declaration of Independence next to having Jefferson and the Second Continental Congress explain it themselves. Lincoln clarified what both Chief Justice Roger Taney and Senator Stephen Douglas misunderstood about the Declaration, explaining both what the founders meant and what they did not mean, especially regarding its claims about human equality and individual rights. He began by observing that though the *Dred Scott* opinion of Taney conceded that "the language of the Declaration is broad enough to include the whole human family," both Taney and Douglas argued that "the authors of that instrument did not intend to include negroes, by the fact that they did not at once, actually place them on an equality with the whites." They judged the founders' professions by their practice: since most of them did not free their slaves upon declaring independence or after establishing their state and national governments, "all men" must not have meant all men regardless of color, race, or ethnicity.[33]

However, Lincoln pointed out that Taney and Douglas were selective in the facts regarding the meaning of equality in the United States. They neglected "the other fact" about the founders: not only did they not make black people equal to white people politically, but "they did not at once, *or ever afterwards*, actually place all white people on an equality with one or another." If practice dictates the meaning of profession, the whole practice must be taken into account. If the right to vote indicates political equality, while it is manifestly true that no mass emancipation and enfranchisement of black people took place in America upon gaining independence from England, no mass or universal enfranchisement of white people occurred either.[34]

Contrary to what he considered the "obvious violence" done by Taney and Douglas to the equality statement of the Declaration, Lincoln argued that its authors "intended to include *all* men, but they did not intend to declare all men equal *in all respects*." When the Declaration's framers "consider[ed] all men created equal," they were not implying equality in "color, size, intellect, moral developments, or social capacity." Instead, they meant "equal in 'certain inalienable rights, among which are life, liberty, and the pursuit of happiness.'" Earlier in his speech, Lincoln used the example of a black woman to argue that while "she certainly is not my equal" in some respects, "in her natural right to eat the bread that she earns with her own hands without asking leave of any one else, she is my equal, and the equal of all others." Lincoln avoided mentioning precisely how a black woman was "certainly" not his equal to focus on the fundamental equality she shared with him and all other human beings: "her natural right" to enjoy the fruit of her own labor. His focus on how they were equal rather than how they differed reminded his audience of the purpose of government according to the Declaration of Independence—namely, to secure what all human beings possess by nature, which are the equal rights to life, liberty, and the pursuit of happiness.[35]

Lincoln repeated this argument in his first formal debate with Stephen Douglas in the 1858 campaign for U.S. Senate. After affirming that black people are just as "entitled" as white people "to all the natural rights enumerated in the Declaration of Independence," he acknowledged that a black man "is not my equal in many respects— certainly not in color, perhaps not in moral or intellectual endowment." Drawing from his experience as a trial lawyer, he conceded the minor point regarding difference in skin color (and hazarded some hesitation about superiority of morals or intelligence) to land the major point: "But in the right to eat the bread, without leave of anybody else, which his own hand earns, *he is my equal and the equal of Judge Douglas, and the equal of every living man.*"[36] In short, as a matter of right, it did not matter in what respects the black woman was not the equal of the white man. As Jefferson once wrote regarding what nature had given black people, "Whatever be their degree of talent it is no measure of their rights. Because Sir Isaac Newton was superior to others in understanding, he was not therefore lord of the person or property of others." The natural rights of black people, just like those of white people, belonged to no one but themselves.[37]

Lincoln then pointed out what should have been obvious as a matter of history but, more important, as a matter of principle: the authors of the Declaration did not claim "that all were then actually enjoying that equality, nor yet, that they were about to confer it immediately upon them." After all, it was a *declaration*, words expressing an opinion regarding the legitimacy of a political course of action. Those words set out facts and a standard by which those facts should be interpreted and acted on. The declaration of their mistreatment by King George III and the principles by which that mistreatment could be readily identified was not a declaration that they had already established a just form of government that secured what they lacked when under the putative authority of England. In Lincoln's words, the founders "had no power to confer such a boon." If they did, there would be no need for the Declaration. "They meant simply to declare the *right*," Lincoln explained, "so that the *enforcement* of it might follow as fast as circumstances should permit."[38] What was true for every human being was their natural possession of rights. What was left for those human beings to do was to erect governments to enforce those rights.

Given the "circumstances" of a war for independence that took several years before victory was ensured, the "enforcement" of everyone's natural rights would not happen immediately. As a new nation working to establish its free and independent status in the world, the conception of natural rights and how best to secure them was still working its way through the population at large. Lincoln believed the founders "meant to set up a standard maxim for free society, which should be familiar to all, and revered by all; constantly looked to, constantly labored for, and even though never perfectly attained, constantly approximated." Over time and through practice, Americans would experience the Declaration "constantly spreading and deepening its influence, and augmenting the happiness and value of life to all people of all colors everywhere." For Lincoln, the founders understood the implications of the self-evident truths of the Declaration not only for King George III but also for themselves. To justify their independence from England and "assume among the powers of the earth, the separate and equal station to which the laws of nature and of nature's God entitle them" (as the Declaration put it), the founding generation was obligated to act consistently with the very principles by which they justified their separation from England.[39]

Their failure to do so immediately with regard to enslaved black people on American soil led Stephen Douglas to misread the Declaration's principles as true only for white people. Lincoln bemoaned "what a mere wreck—mangled ruin" Douglas made of "our once glorious Declaration." Claiming the founders intended to apply its equality principle only to white people, Douglas robbed the Declaration of its noblest truth. According to Douglas, "They were speaking of British subjects on this continent being equal to British subjects born and residing in Great Britain." Lincoln could not abide this misinterpretation of the Declaration: "I had thought the Declaration promised something better than the condition of British subjects; but no, it only meant that we should be equal to them in their own oppressed and unequal condition." To allow the Declaration to "be thus frittered away" and "thus left no more at most, than an interesting memorial of the dead past," would rob it "of its vitality, and practical value; and left without the *germ* or even the *suggestion* of the individual rights of man in it." Lincoln was unequivocal in his reading the equality statement of the Declaration to include all human beings, regardless of race. "I should like to know if taking this old Declaration of Independence, which declares that all men are equal upon principle and making exceptions to it where will it stop. If one man says it does not mean a negro, why not another say it does not mean some other man?" He observed in 1858, "I believe each individual is naturally entitled to do as he please with himself and the fruit of his labor, so far as it in no wise interferes with any other man's rights." Lincoln insisted that the equal rights of humanity admitted of no exceptions: all human beings possessed natural rights or none did, and he believed that this was the understanding of the founders when they declared it as the basis of their new nation.[40]

Speaking in Baltimore in April 1864, Lincoln discussed the debated concept of liberty: "The world has never had a good definition of the word liberty, and the American people, just now, are much in want of one." He noted that what people meant by it differed according to their own self-interest: "We all declare for liberty; but in using the same *word* we do not all mean the same *thing*. With some the word liberty may mean for each man to do as he pleases with himself, and the product of his labor; while with others the same word may mean for some men to do as they please with other men, and the product of other men's labor." There would not have been a war but for this disagreement over defining a word that was so important and central in the American political lexicon, a disagreement that led to violence over what each side considered "liberty and tyranny." Given that Maryland was moving to abolish slavery in its constitution, Lincoln congratulated the state for practically defining liberty as the natural possession of both white and black people. Channeling his inner Aesop, he used a sheep and a wolf to contrast the opposing definitions of liberty currently at stake in the Civil War: "The shepherd drives the wolf from the sheep's throat, for which the sheep thanks the shepherd as a *liberator*, while the wolf denounces him for the same act as the destroyer of liberty, especially as the sheep was a black one." With Maryland's decision to propose a new state constitution that abolished slavery (which it eventually approved on October 13, 1864), Lincoln concluded that "the wolf's dictionary, has been repudiated."[41]

Consent

> What I do say is, that no man is good enough to govern another man, *without that other's consent*. I say this is the leading principle—the sheet anchor of American republicanism.
> —Abraham Lincoln, Speech at Peoria, Illinois (1854)

If all human beings are created equal, endowed by their Creator with the same rights as everyone else, then it follows logically that the only legitimate way to rule anyone is by that person's permission. Consent is the flip side of the equality coin, because no one is the natural ruler of anyone but himself. For a political community, consent is both the way that civil society is formed out of naturally self-governing individuals and the basis of its operation once government is established. Enlightenment political philosophers called this the social contract, and it was the fundamental basis of Lincoln's understanding of human beings and society.[42]

The clearest expression of Lincoln's devotion to the consent principle of the Declaration is found in his seminal Peoria Address of 1854. In it he criticized the Kansas-Nebraska Act for permitting slavery's expansion into territory where the 1820 Missouri Compromise had declared "slavery and involuntary servitude . . . forever prohibited." This possibility arose under the act's policy of popular sovereignty or congressional "nonintervention," the signature doctrine of the bill's sponsor, Stephen A. Douglas. The Kansas-Nebraska Act intended "not to legislate slavery into any Territory or State, nor to exclude it therefrom, but to leave the people thereof perfectly free to form and regulate their domestic institutions in their own way." Lincoln found the act defective on a number of counts but emphasized its moral deficiency due to its "*declared* indifference" to the prospect of slavery entering federal territory. Contrary to Douglas's popular sovereignty, which implied "no right principle of action but *self-interest*," the Declaration of Independence taught that all human beings are "endowed by their Creator with certain unalienable Rights," and that governments derive "their just powers from the consent of the governed." Lincoln believed the Declaration's great lesson was that "no man is good enough to govern another man, *without that other's consent*. I say this is the leading principle—the sheet anchor of American republicanism."[43]

Lincoln borrowed the phrase "sheet anchor" from Thomas Jefferson's First Inaugural Address. Where Jefferson called the federal government "the sheet anchor of our peace at home and safety abroad," Lincoln was more specific in using "sheet anchor" to indicate that the strongest security of a free people is the principle of consent. He then quoted directly and emphatically from the Declaration's second paragraph: "DERIVING THEIR JUST POWERS FROM THE CONSENT OF THE GOVERNED." Because Stephen Douglas frequently referred to his policy of popular sovereignty as "the great principle of self-government," Lincoln insisted on correcting his use of the term: "Allow ALL the governed an equal voice in the government, and that, and that only, is self-government."[44]

In his famous "House Divided" speech, when Lincoln accepted the unanimous nomination of the Republican Party to campaign against Stephen Douglas in 1858, he returned to this question of popular sovereignty rightly understood. He agreed with Douglas that it should be considered a "sacred right of self government," because it expressed "the only rightful basis of any government." However, as Douglas reserved it for white people only, Lincoln thought it had become "so perverted in this attempted use of it as to amount to just this: That if any *one* man, choose to enslave *another*, no *third* man shall be allowed to object."[45] He showed how Douglas's popular sovereignty corrupted the true principle of consent by permitting the enslavement of black people as long as a white majority supported it. Douglas interpreted the Constitution to allow "the people of every State the right to have slavery or not have it . . . as they choose, each State being left free to decide for itself." The consent of black people was not necessary, for he considered them an inferior race of human beings. Douglas summed up the difference between Lincoln and himself by saying that Lincoln "looks forward to a time when slavery shall be abolished everywhere. I look forward to a time when each State shall be allowed to do as it pleases." As long as white Americans were free to determine the extent of black freedom, Douglas was satisfied that he was following what "our fathers" had originally established.[46]

Douglas liked to add that the white race should not abuse its political authority over the black race but should act with common decency. As he put it, "I hold that humanity and christianity both require that the negro shall have and enjoy every right, every privilege, and every immunity consistent with the safety of the society in which he lives." To those who wondered what rights, privileges, and immunities black people deserved to have protected on American soil, Douglas replied, "This is a question which each State and each Territory must decide for itself." He noted that black people in Illinois were neither slaves nor first-class citizens. White Illinoisans protected a black resident "in his civil rights, in his life, his person and his property, only depriving him of all political rights whatsoever, and refusing to put him on an equality with the white man." In sum, Douglas was a legal positivist, believing that the rights of so-called inferior races were determined not by God or nature but by governments run exclusively by the popular majority of white citizens.[47]

Throughout his debates with Douglas, Lincoln showed white Illinoisans that their own right to be ruled only by consent would be undermined if they allowed white settlers in Kansas to rule black people without consent: "Now, when by all these means you have succeeded in dehumanizing the negro; when you have put him down, and made it forever impossible for him to be but as the beasts of the field . . . are you quite sure the demon which you have roused *will not turn and rend you*?" Lincoln showed them that the exercise of majority political might against the black minority in Illinois could become a double-edged sword. He thought the founders pointed to a better, more secure, principle than color or race as the basis of popular government, asking, "What constitutes the bulwark of our own liberty and independence?" Not arms or soldiers but an idea, a timeless, universal truth: "Our reliance is in the *love of liberty* which God has planted in our bosoms. Our defense is in the preservation of the spirit which prizes liberty as the heritage of all men, in all lands, every where." If all men were not created equal, if liberty was not the natural possession of every human being, then numerical might and not natural right would set the boundary of who ruled and who got ruled. Lincoln thus concluded, "Familiarize yourselves with the chains of bondage, and you are preparing your own limbs to wear them. Accustomed to trample on the rights of those around you, you have lost the genius of your own independence, and become the fit subjects of the first cunning tyrant who rises." In this way, Lincoln tried to show how the expansion of black slavery into the western territories of the United States could lead to the enslavement of white people.[48]

The key to the protection of the rights of white people in America depended on their conviction that those rights belonged to all human beings. For Lincoln, that meant shoring up their belief in the humanity of black people. In protecting the rights of those considered the least and most vulnerable in their community, they would accustom themselves to protecting the rights of any who found themselves outnumbered in the political process and hence vulnerable to the majority in power. As Thomas Jefferson explained in his First Inaugural Address, "Though the will of the majority is in all cases to prevail, that will, to be rightful, must be reasonable; that the minority possess their equal rights, which equal laws must protect, and to violate would be oppression." The rights of the minority are the same rights possessed by the majority—the rights of the individual. By standing up for the individual rights of black Americans, Lincoln was teaching white Americans how to defend their own rights.[49]

Consent became a practical concern for Lincoln after his election to the presidency. In between his election and inauguration, citizens of seven slaveholding states decided that a Republican president would not protect their interests, and therefore they claimed the right to secede from the United States. In response, Lincoln explained the necessity of accepting the outcome of elections—the concrete expression of consent—regardless of who won or lost. In December 1860, Lincoln rejected calls for compromise to avoid secession and the dissolution of the Union: "Is it desired that I shall shift the ground upon which I have been elected? I can not do it." As president-elect, Lincoln did not address most policy matters before he assumed office. He thought he deserved to fulfill his election promises and those of his party. To do otherwise, he added, "would make me appear as if I repented for the crime of having been elected, and was anxious to apologize and beg forgiveness." Most important, he highlighted the central plank of his party platform, as it addressed the central issue of the 1860 election: "On the territorial question, I am inflexible. . . . You think slavery is right and ought to be extended; we think it is wrong and ought to be restricted." Lincoln had not changed his mind since his 1858 debates with Douglas, so he directed the attention of critics to the written record, fearing that to say anything more would invite deliberate misinterpretations and thus exacerbate the divisions then pressing the nation.[50]

As he traveled to the White House for his inauguration, he avoided speaking at length about how he would address attempts at secession. However, he highlighted instructive examples of obedience to the Constitution and laws. For example, on February 21, 1861, the New Jersey State Senate hosted a reception for the president-elect, even though a majority were Democrats who had voted for Lincoln's Illinois rival, Stephen Douglas, for president. New Jersey allowed its seven electoral votes for president to be divided among the leading candidates, with four Republican electors voting for Lincoln and three Democratic electors voting for Stephen Douglas. With the secession of seven states by February 1, 1861, Lincoln's decision to stop at the New Jersey state capitol was intended to show his appreciation of citizens who, despite having voted for another candidate, chose to honor Lincoln's election to the nation's highest office.

He closed his brief remarks by calling attention to the polite reception the New Jersey Senate gave him "without distinction of party." Lincoln valued this nonpartisan respect by men who, regardless of their votes, abided by the election of a Republican president. He remarked, "I learn that this body is composed of a majority of gentlemen who, in the exercise of their best judgment in the choice of a Chief Magistrate, did not think I was the man." Nevertheless, he noted, they received him "as the constitutional President of the United States—as citizens of the United States, to meet the man who, for the time being, is the representative man of the nation, united by a purpose to perpetuate the Union and liberties of the people." Self-government could not last without self-control on the part of the citizenry, which at minimum required obedience to lawfully elected officials. In particular, government by consent of the governed required that political dissent be expressed in constitutional and civil ways, not unconstitutional or violent ones. The New Jersey senators demonstrated how to be good losers. Lincoln would soon explain in his First Inaugural Address how he intended to be a good winner.[51]

In a letter to a Pennsylvania congressman who proposed several amendments and laws as concessions to the South, Lincoln laid out in plain terms why abiding by the election, and brooking no immediate compromises, was fundamental to the operation of a free society: "We have just carried an election on principles fairly stated to the people. . . . [I]f we surrender, it is the end of us, and of the government. They will repeat the experiment upon us *ad libitum*." For Lincoln and the Republican Party to give in to the losing party, the southern faction of Breckenridge Democrats, would undermine the whole point of voting. It would grant the losers of an election veto power over the main goals and policies on which the winning party had won the election. Instead of reflecting the will of the majority, popular consent would become tyranny by the minority. Lincoln thought that would be an absurd precedent to set for the only self-governing nation in the world.[52]

In his July 4, 1861, Message to Congress in Special Session, with the Civil War under way, Lincoln acknowledged that compromises sometimes were fitting. However, in this instance, "no popular government can long survive a marked precedent, that those who carry an election, can only save the government from immediate destruction, by giving up the main point, upon which the people gave the election." If the American people believed the new president had failed to work with Congress to rule in the interest of all Americans, Lincoln concluded that the citizenry and not public officials could "safely reverse their own deliberate decisions." Lincoln defended the sanctity of the electoral process by abiding by those "deliberate decisions" and administering the government by defending it from its enemies, not by yielding to them.[53]

He acknowledged that "the people may err in an election." However, Lincoln explained, "the true cure is in the next election; and not in the treachery of the party elected." This was precisely how the Republican Party proceeded when it failed to elect John C. Frémont president in November 1856. Instead of being sore losers, Republicans accepted the election of the Democratic president, James Buchanan, and acted like good losers by remaining in the American Union. They employed the peaceful means of the political process by redoubling their efforts to shape public opinion and campaigned in 1858 and 1860 to elect Republicans to state and national offices. Republicans believed that in America, as in any self-governing society, their political philosophy must be "If at first you don't succeed, try, try again." Try again they did, and with the help of a Democratic Party divided into Northern and Southern factions, the Republicans became a controlling majority in the House of Representatives in 1860, gained seats in the Senate, and elected Abraham Lincoln president. With the firing on the federal garrison at Fort Sumter by Confederate batteries in Charleston, South Carolina, a civil war began less than two months after Lincoln's inauguration. This threatened to show that free people were incapable of governing by their own consent.[54]

Right of Revolution

Any people anywhere, being inclined and having the power, have the *right* to rise up, and shake off the existing government, and form a new one that suits them better. This is a most valuable,—a most sacred right—a right, which we hope and believe, is to liberate the world.

—Abraham Lincoln, Speech in United States House of Representatives: The War with Mexico (1848)

The most sobering of the rights associated with the Declaration of Independence is the right of revolution. According to the Declaration, whenever any government fails to secure the rights of the governed, "it is the Right of the People to alter or to abolish it, and to institute new Government, laying its foundation on such principles and organizing its powers in such form, as to them shall seem most likely to effect their Safety and Happiness." The people's right to "alter or abolish" their government when it goes astray does not depend on the express terms of a constitution or permission of those in power. It is a natural right and therefore one that serves as a last resort for an oppressed people and a tacit check on government misrule.[55]

As a congressman, Lincoln made explicit reference to this right in the controversy over the Mexican-American War. With the war with Mexico winding down, he criticized President James Polk for starting it without just cause. Lincoln highlighted the alleged border or "spot" where Polk claimed that Americans were killed by the Mexican government, which was Polk's justification for the war. Mexico claimed control over territory up to the eastern bank of the Rio Grande, and Texas claimed control over territory up to the western bank of the Nueces River. Lincoln later argued that "the uninhabited country between the two . . . depended, not on any *treaty-fixed* boundary (for no treaty had attempted it) but on revolution." He put the matter directly: "Any portion of such people that *can, may* revolutionize, and make their *own*, of so much of the teritory as they inhabit." He then defined revolution for his colleagues in the House of Representatives with a paraphrase of the Declaration of Independence: "Any people anywhere, being inclined and having the power, have the *right* to rise up, and shake off the existing government, and form a new one that suits them better." Lincoln called this right "a most valuable,—a most sacred right—a right, which we hope and believe, is to liberate the world." Lincoln believed the right of revolution could bring forth liberty because it was a natural right, the possession of any people determined to be free, like the citizens of Texas who had exercised it against Mexico. Where Texas had "carried her revolution, by obtaining the *actual*, willing or unwilling, submission of the people, *so far*, the country was hers, and no farther." He doubted, however, that the Texans had exercised authority in the territory between the Rio Grande and the Nueces River. Thus, Polk had begun an unconstitutional and unjust war over territory not under the jurisdiction of the United States.[56]

In claiming a constitutional right to secede, white Southerners argued they were not rebelling or exercising a natural right of revolution. Instead, they insisted, they were constitutionally acting to reassert their sovereign authority as a result of the illegitimate actions of other members of the federal Union. Interpreting the Constitution as a compact of states—like a league or alliance—rather than a national government, they justified secession as an official acknowledgment that the national compact had been broken. Therefore, they maintained, political authority had returned to the citizens of the respective states, whose state governments acted as their agents. South Carolina, the first state to secede, declared that "non-slaveholding States . . . have enacted laws which either nullify the Acts of Congress or render useless any attempt to execute them," by which it meant passage of "personal liberty" laws that disrupted the enforcement of the Fugitive Slave Act of 1850. Because "the constituted compact has been deliberately broken and disregarded by the non-slaveholding states, . . . the consequence follows that South Carolina is released from her obligation." Ten of the remaining fourteen slaveholding states followed suit, offering similar reasons for their separation from the United States.[57]

In his First Inaugural Address, Lincoln rejected this view of the Constitution as a compact of states rather than a real national government.

He argued that even if the federal government were more like a league than a real government, no state would have the authority to secede from the American union, because "if the United States be not a government proper, but an association of States in the nature of contract merely, can it, as a contract, be peaceably be unmade, by less than all the parties who made it?" Lincoln went on to argue that because the Constitution really established a national government and not a league or confederation, secession was prohibited because it contradicted the practical operation of self-government.[58]

"Plainly, the central idea of secession," Lincoln stated, "is the essence of anarchy." The word *anarchy* means without rule or order. To reject the outcome of an election simply because it was not the outcome one wanted would produce chaos. Instead, Lincoln maintained, "A majority, held in restraint by constitutional checks, and limitations, and always changing easily, with deliberate changes of popular opinions and sentiments, is the only true sovereign of a free people." Self-government, or popular sovereignty rightly understood, recognizes that while the majority has authority to rule, it must protect the rights it shares with the minority. Moreover, constitutional checks and balances keep the majority from becoming tyrannical in its exercise of political power and thereby gives the minority no legitimate cause for exercising the natural right of revolution.[59]

After elections facilitate a "contest of opinion," Thomas Jefferson observed, producing a result "decided by the voice of the nation, announced according to the rules of the constitution," it becomes incumbent on all to "arrange themselves under the will of the law, and unite in common efforts for the common good."[60] This is what Lincoln meant by "always changing easily, with deliberate changes of popular opinions and sentiments." To do otherwise with no reasonable cause would transform freedom into lawlessness. Therefore, secession was not a reasonable option for a loss at the polls. As president-elect, Lincoln noted "that no state can, in any way lawfully, get out of the Union, without the consent of the others," and that it was "the duty of the President, and other government functionaries to run the machine as it is." To permit Americans to refuse to abide by the results of a national election by allowing their separation from the Union would subvert the rule of law and prove that "popular government" was unworkable. Lincoln called this "disintegration," deeming it a "principle . . . upon which no government can possibly endure." Only if the people willingly obeyed the government, which entailed abiding by the outcome of free elections, could they demonstrate the viability of self-government.[61]

After the surrender of Fort Sumter, Lincoln called out the militia "to suppress said combinations, and to cause the laws to be duly executed," and convened Congress to meet in special session on July 4 "to consider and determine, such measures, as, in their wisdom, the public safety, and interest may seem to demand." He called on "all loyal citizens to favor, facilitate and aid this effort to maintain the honor, the integrity, and the existence of our National Union, and the perpetuity of popular government." How Americans decided to respond not only to a divisive election but also to the subsequent attempt at secession would determine the fate of self-government. With the bombing of a federal fort, that response would require a war to defend a self-governing way of life. As he put it in his message to Congress in that special session, "It is now for them to demonstrate to the world, that those who can fairly carry an election, can also suppress a rebellion—that ballots are the rightful, and peaceful, successors of bullets; and that when ballots have fairly, and constitutionally, decided, there can be no successful appeal, back to bullets." In Lincoln's mind, secession was rebellion, and a free people had no choice but to quell the internal attempt at disrupting the peaceful process of constitutional self-rule.[62]

He went on to explain that the leaders of the secession movement in the South deliberately chose not to use the language of revolution in their attempt to establish a separate country. Most white Southerners would not have joined the effort to separate as an exercise in revolution or rebellion because they "possessed as much of moral sense, as much of devotion to law and order, and as much pride in, and reverence for, the history, and government, of their common country, as any other civilized, and patriotic people." Secession leaders "knew they could never raise their treason to any respectable magnitude, by any name which implies *violation* of law." As Lincoln saw it, "They commenced by an insidious debauching of the public mind" by arguing that a state could withdraw from the Union peacefully and lawfully without gaining the consent of the other states. He then put the matter plainly: "With rebellion thus sugar-coated, they have been drugging the public mind of their section for more than thirty years." By the time of Lincoln's election, Southerners who thought his administration could not be trusted to protect their interests had been taught to view secession as a legitimate remedy under the Constitution. However, Lincoln understood true consent to require obedience to the Constitution and laws, with the exception of revolution justified if government had clearly violated the rights of the people.[63]

Self-Improvement

> I want every man to have the chance—and I believe a black man is entitled to it—in which he *can* better his condition—when he may look forward and hope to be a hired laborer this year and the next, work for himself afterward, and finally to hire men to work for him! That is the true system.
>
> —Abraham Lincoln, Speech at New Haven, Connecticut (1860)

Lincoln was a firm believer in self-improvement, which he derived from the concepts of human equality and individual rights. If the individual rights of all people were protected equally in civil society, then they would have an incentive to work hard, knowing they would enjoy the fruits of their labor. Lincoln put the matter simply: "Property is the fruit of labor—property is desirable—is a positive good in the world." He explained the incentive everyone had to work hard even when only a few prospered greatly under the protection of private property: "That some should be rich, shows that others may become rich, and hence is just encouragement to industry and enterprize. Let not him who is houseless pull down the house of another; but let him labor diligently and build one for himself, thus by example assuring that his own shall be safe from violence when built." Lincoln showed the power of incentive and secure hope in encouraging industry, productivity, and prosperity. Where property is protected by government and respected by the people, all are given due motivation to labor for themselves to reap the rewards of their labor. The cultivation of individual talents and the development of skills and expertise would lead to the cultivation of both land and men, thereby generating a prosperous nation unlike any that the world had ever known. Here Lincoln preached what he had long been practicing.[64]

Unlike Stephen Douglas, who claimed that the Declaration of Independence applied only to white Americans, Lincoln believed "the Declaration contemplated the progressive improvement in the condition of all men everywhere." He thought the principles of human equality and individual rights invited any race of people to improve their lot in life. As counterexamples, Lincoln cited the British monarchy and Southern slavery as political systems that thwarted productivity when compared with the prosperity owing to "the free institutions of our country." He therefore maintained that the cause of America's success was "that every man can make himself." For Lincoln, "every man" included black people.[65]

Among the many tragedies of slavery was the deprivation of an opportunity to improve oneself. When Lincoln criticized popular sovereignty for its tendency to encourage the spread of slavery, he noted this impact on enslaved black people in America: "I combat it as having a tendency to dehumanize the negro—to take away from him the right of ever striving to be a man." Responding to an inquiry about his opinion of a waiting period for voting by naturalized citizens in Massachusetts, Lincoln answered, "Understanding the spirit of our institutions to aim at the *elevation* of men, I am opposed to whatever tends to *degrade* them." Lincoln noted that he had become associated with the elevation of black people through his debates with Stephen Douglas: "I have some little notoriety for commiserating the oppressed condition of the negro; and I should be strangely inconsistent if I could favor any project for curtailing the existing rights of *white men*, even though born in different lands, and speaking different languages from myself." In a letter to his junior law partner, William Herndon, Lincoln stated, "The way for a young man to rise, is to improve himself every way he can, never suspecting that any body wishes to hinder him." In a note to himself about the power of hope to inspire hard work, Lincoln wrote, "Free labor has the inspiration of hope; pure slavery has no hope. The power of hope upon human exertion, and happiness, is wonderful." He added that even some slave masters make use of the concept of hope to improve productivity: "The slave whom you can not drive with the lash to break seventy-five pounds of hemp in a day, if you will task him to break a hundred, and promise him pay for all he does over, he will break you a hundred and fifty." When one "substituted hope, for the rod," personal development and economic prosperity was sure to follow.[66]

In a note to himself, Lincoln observed that most governments denied individual rights, whereas the United States affirmed them, and the results told the tale: "*They* said, some men are too *ignorant*, and *vicious*, to share in government. Possibly so, said we; and, by your system, you would always keep them ignorant, and vicious." Not so in America: "We proposed to give *all* a chance; and we expected the weak to grow stronger, the ignorant, wiser; and all better, and happier together." Lincoln concluded that government "denial of equal rights of men" impeded human development, whereas American self-government allowed people to better themselves. Here he adopted the white supremacist logic of Southern slave owners only to demonstrate that the truly American way was to afford all an equal chance in the race of life. Lincoln used their assumption that the black race was inferior to show that by their system of oppression, enslaved black people were guaranteed not to improve themselves, whereas by the system of freedom practiced in the North, no one was destined to remain in a low estate.[67]

Most white Illinoisans possessed the pervasive racial bigotry of their time, so Lincoln developed an argument against slavery grounded on simple fairness. "Suppose it is true, that the negro is inferior to the white, in the gifts of nature," Lincoln noted to himself, "is it not the exact reverse justice that the white should, for that reason, take from the negro, any part of the little which has been given him?" Instead, "'Give to him that is needy' is the christian rule of charity;

but 'Take from him that is needy' is the rule of slavery." Whether one consulted the plain dictates of justice or the divine command of the Christian religion, Lincoln believed the answer for the typical white Northerner would be the same. Even presuming black inferiority, the decent, Christian attitude should be one of sympathetic respect and generosity toward one's presumed inferiors.[68]

Lincoln's opposition to slavery was equaled by his belief in equal opportunity. As he told New England audiences in March 1860, "When one starts poor, as most do in the race of life, free society is such that he knows he can better his condition; he knows that there is no fixed condition of labor, for his whole life." Here Lincoln spoke from experience. "I am not ashamed to confess that twenty five years ago I was a hired laborer, mauling rails, at work on a flat-boat—just what might happen to any poor man's son!" He then connected his own experience of improving his lot in life with the freedom he thought every person should have: "I want every man to have the chance—and I believe a black man is entitled to it—in which he *can* better his condition." This theme of free labor inducing people to work hard and cultivate what they had in terms of innate ability and material resources was one he developed extensively in an 1859 speech at a state fair in Wisconsin. There he called free labor "the just and generous, and prosperous system, which opens the way for all—gives hope to all, and energy, and progress, and improvement of condition to all." Lincoln observed that "as the Author of man makes every individual with one head and one pair of hands, it was probably intended that heads and hands should co-operate as friends; and that that particular head, should direct and control that particular pair of hands." To reinforce this clear refutation of the principle of slavery, Lincoln added "that each head is the natural guardian, director, and protector of the hands and mouth inseparably connected with it," and hence "every head should be cultivated, and improved, by whatever will add to its capacity for performing its charge."[69]

Given Lincoln's own rise from poverty to affluence, the obligation of every free person to improve his or her lot in life was no mere theory for him. It was a lesson he attempted, with little success, to convey to his ne'er-do-well stepbrother, John D. Johnston. Lincoln explained that the cause of Johnston's poverty had nothing to do with where he lived and everything to do with his failure to apply himself. When Johnston wanted to sell the family plot and try his luck in Missouri, Lincoln wrote to him with a candor just short of a family intervention: "You have raised no crop this year, and what you really want is to sell the land, get the money and spend it—part with the land you have, and my life upon it, you will never after, own a spot big enough to bury you in." Lincoln's proposal? "*Go to work* is the only cure for your case." His frank letter came a few years after another episode where Johnston asked Lincoln to loan him eighty dollars. Lincoln reminded him that he had not repaid earlier loans, which had never kept Johnston from falling back into debt. He wrote that this was entirely due to "some defect in your *conduct*. What that defect is I think I know. You are not *lazy*, and still you *are* an *idler*. I doubt whether since I saw you, you have done a good whole day's work in any one day." Lincoln followed this blunt appraisal with a proposition that he hoped would be the hand up that proved better than a handout: "To secure you a fair reward for your labor, I now promise you, that for every dollar you will, between this and the first of next May, get for your own labor, either in money, or in your own indebtedness, I will then give you one other dollar." Lincoln added that this arrangement would not only improve his financial situation but, more important, also improve his character: "Now if you will do this, you will soon be out of debt, and what is better, you will have a habit that will keep you from getting in debt again." The fact that Johnston's own children would be witnesses of this new approach to providing for himself and his family, Lincoln commented, would be "more important to them, because they have longer to live, and can keep out of an idle habit before they are in it; easier than they can get out after they are in." His proposition, needless to say, fell on deaf ears.[70]

Johnston's failure to make something of himself was a sore disappointment to Lincoln. Less than a year apart in age, they were reared in the same hardscrabble frontier of Kentucky and Indiana as youngsters in a mixed family. Referring to his own meager upbringing in a campaign autobiography, Lincoln observed, "There is not much of it, for the reason, I suppose, that there is not much of me."[71] But in a country where the fruit of one's labor—especially for white people—was protected by law, Lincoln saw and frequently took note of the abiding incentive to work hard and improve one's lot in life. He had tried a number of occupations before establishing a law practice. Lincoln alluded to this "right to rise" a few years after becoming president: "I happen temporarily to occupy this big White House. I am a living witness that any one of your children may look to come here as my father's child has." He cited this freedom to rise as high as one's efforts could take one, what he called "our birthright" and "inestimable jewel," as a motive for fighting the war: "It is in order that each of you may have through this free government which we have enjoyed, an open field and a fair chance for your industry, enterprise and intelligence; that you may all have equal privileges in the race of life, with all its desirable human aspirations." In the founding principles of human equality and individual rights, and a government established to protect the fruits of that liberty, Lincoln saw the greatest hope for a poor person to aspire to "the highest privileges and positions." He thought, "Nowhere in the world is presented a government of so much liberty and equality." Lincoln preached what he had already practiced in his own life: starting in a position of social and economic inferiority, he worked his way up the social and economic ladder. Lincoln believed that if he could improve his lot in life, so could others, but only if Americans stuck by the principle of human equality and its corollary practice of equal protection of the laws. In so doing, those with sufficient resolution, ambition, education, and training could reap the rewards of their labor.[72]

In his 1861 Message to Congress in Special Session, Lincoln described the Civil War as "essentially a People's contest." He described the defense of the American union as "a struggle for maintaining in the world, that form, and substance of government, whose leading object is, to elevate the condition of men—to lift artificial weights from all shoulders—to clear the paths of laudable pursuit for all—to afford all, an unfettered start, and a fair chance, in the race of life." Victory for the Union meant victory for a type of government that secured for its citizens the fruits of their labor. By winning the war, loyal Americans could show citizens of other nations how to secure their own freedom and thereby improve their own lives by following the Americans' example.[73]

* * *

As the foregoing sections demonstrated, Lincoln found the key to American prosperity in the ideals of the Declaration of Independence. By their application, he could trace his own rise from social obscurity to the nation's highest political station. While he made frequent reference to "rights" in his four terms as an Illinois state representative (1834–42), only rarely did he quote or cite the Declaration by name. While there was no serious threat of slavery's expansion in the 1830s, Lincoln had little reason to cite the Declaration during his tenure in the Illinois Statehouse. His most explicit appeals to the Declaration and its antislavery principles came during the 1850s and the early years of the Civil War, when he endeavored to shape public opinion on the most pressing question of the day: whether slavery should be permitted to expand into federal territory. Before his election as president, Lincoln said, "I have always hated slavery, I think as much as any Abolitionist." He explained that he had "always been quiet about it" until the threat of slavery's expansion arose with Stephen Douglas's Nebraska Bill in 1859. He added that as long as most Americans "rested in the belief that slavery was in course of ultimate extinction," he too would keep quiet about it."[74]

However, when the Mexican-American War vastly increased the western frontier of the United States, the status of slavery in those territories became an unavoidable issue. Lincoln's relative silence about the 1850 Compromise measures after he left Congress in 1849 indicated that he thought the threat of secession at that time had passed. But as he noted in an 1859 campaign autobiography, "I was losing interest in politics, when the repeal of the Missouri Compromise aroused me again." The Kansas-Nebraska Act repealed the 1820 Missouri Compromise and opened territory north of the 36°30' parallel to slavery if settlers there wanted it. Lincoln returned to politics to prevent the extension of slavery, and he drew on the principles of the Declaration of Independence to remind white citizens of the basis of their own rights as they debated the future of black slavery on American soil. The political principles of the founders indicated not only the ends to which any legitimate regime should be devoted but also the means to those ends. The next chapter examines the implementation of those political means—the federal Constitution and union of American states—and Lincoln's consistent appeals to the Constitution as the fundamental way for Americans to fulfill the ends spelled out in the Declaration of Independence.[75]

LINCOLN AND THE
CONSTITUTION: AN APPEAL
TO THE FOUNDERS' MEANS

Don't interfere with anything in the Constitution. That must be maintained, for it is the only safeguard of our liberties.
—Abraham Lincoln, Speech at Kalamazoo, Michigan (1856)

If the Declaration of Independence explains the ends of the American regime, then the U.S. Constitution spells out the means. To be sure, the state governments formed during the revolutionary period acted most directly to secure the rights of the governed. Nevertheless, if the revolution proved anything, it showed Americans that regardless of which state they inhabited, a unity of the American states would be necessary to achieve independence. Moreover, without that political unity, individual liberty would not be protected for long. However, despite helping unite Americans in critical moments of their early existence as one people, neither the Second Continental Congress nor the Articles of Confederation and Perpetual Union could meet the ends set forth in the Declaration. These political means became obsolete after further experience and reflection convinced them that they needed a stronger federal government. They designed the U.S. Constitution to provide a stronger national government for purposes affecting all the American states, while maintaining state and local governments for matters within each state. Slavery within those states would pose the greatest challenge to maintaining the union of the American states under a federal constitution.

Lincoln believed that respect for the Constitution required an adherence to federalism even though the rights of the states to order their own internal affairs would prevent the federal government from banning slavery where it already existed. He understood that constitutional compromises over slavery were necessary to maintain a United States of America. Nevertheless, Lincoln observed that although Congress was not allowed to abolish slavery in the states, the framers permitted Congress to cut off the slave trade into the American union after a period of twenty years (which it did). Congress also prohibited slavery in the Northwest Territory, which was the only territory the United States possessed at the time. Lincoln saw these efforts to cut off the supply and prevent slavery's expansion as constitutional steps toward the eventual eradication of slavery. He appealed to this approach of the founders as the most prudent way for his generation to address the increasing agitation over slavery and thought the Constitution was indispensable to securing the ends of the Declaration of Independence.

The preamble to the Constitution announces several aims, the first and last of which are to "form a more perfect union" and "secure the blessings of liberty." Lincoln explained the connection between the means of constitutional union and the end of liberty in a note to himself after receiving a letter in December 1860 from Alexander H. Stephens, the future vice president of the Confederate States of America. Stephens and Lincoln were fellow Whigs when Lincoln served in the House of Representatives from 1847 to 1849. A week after Lincoln's election on November 6, 1860, Stephens spoke against secession before the Georgia legislature. He then wrote to the president-elect on December 22, "Do what you can to save our common country." Quoting Proverbs 25:11, Stephens suggested, "A word fitly spoken by you now would be like 'apples of gold in pictures of silver.'"[1] Lincoln suspected that any new statement from him would simply be misconstrued and exacerbate the national crisis. He therefore had decided not to give any speech clarifying his positions on slavery, secession, or the fugitive slave law before his March 4 inauguration.[2]

But reflecting on Stephens's reference to Proverbs 25, Lincoln concluded that what the nation needed most was not new words from him but old words found in the Declaration of Independence. Lincoln's note showed that as important as the Constitution and union were, they existed to fulfill the ends mentioned in the Declaration.

Lincoln had read a newspaper account of Stephens's speech to the Georgia legislature and wrote to him for a copy. In that November 14, 1860, speech, Stephens highlighted the state's "unrivalled prosperity in the Union" as a reason to stay in the Union. Given Georgia's significant exports of cotton, he pointed to the state's "foreign trade" as "the foundation of all our prosperity," which owed its increase to "the protection of the navy." In sum, Stephens thought "such rapid progress in the development of wealth, and all the material resources of national power and greatness, as the Southern States have under the general government," they owed to the American union.[3] But where Stephens highlighted the strength of the constitutional union as the sine qua non of American prosperity, Lincoln pointed to a higher cause.

Lincoln acknowledged, "Without the *Constitution* and the *Union*, we could not have attained the result," but added that "even these, are not the primary cause of our great prosperity." He attributed America's success not to a governmental system but to "a philosophical cause," an idea "entwining itself more closely about the human heart." Lincoln thought the Constitution and union existed for the sake of something higher, what he called "the principle of 'Liberty to all.'" Given his frequent verbatim quotations of the Declaration of Independence, especially "all men are created equal," Lincoln's decision to paraphrase the Declaration's equality principle as "Liberty to all" can be explained by the situation the nation faced when he penned this note. By the presidential election of 1860, Americans no longer agreed about what the Constitution empowered Congress to do regarding slavery in the federal territories. This disagreement about the Constitution actually reflected a more fundamental disagreement about the Declaration of Independence, especially its claim about human equality. In fact, secession speeches and ordinances mentioned "equality" not to describe all human beings but to affirm the equal status of states in the federal union. Georgia, for example, feared the incoming Republican administration would "deprive us of an equal enjoyment of the common Territories of the republic." This meant the equal rights of Southern citizens to take their property into federal territory, including their slaves. In his note, Lincoln rephrased the equality principle as "Liberty to all" to make clear that the Declaration considered all human beings equal in their liberty regardless of race.[4]

As Lincoln noted further, "No oppressed, people will *fight*, and *endure*, as our fathers did, without the promise of something better, than a mere change of masters." If liberty belonged to all by nature, then those possessing that liberty had every incentive to erect a government to protect that common possession of each member of the community. It was that principle, Lincoln noted, "that clears the *path* for all—gives *hope* to all—and by consequence, *enterprize*, and *industry* to all." Moreover, the "*expression* of that principle, in our Declaration of Independence," Lincoln called "most happy and fortunate" precisely because it gave incentive to Americans to fight to establish "free government" and their "consequent prosperity."[5]

He continued to expound on the connection between the Declaration and the Constitution: "The assertion of that *principle*, at *that time*, was *the* word, '*fitly spoken*' which has proved an 'apple of gold' to us." Whereas Stephens wanted a word from Lincoln to calm an agitated country, Lincoln believed a word had already been "fitly spoken"—or at least written. The equality principle of the Declaration, written decades earlier, was worth gold to the American people. Lincoln then made clear the hierarchy of means and ends that he found in the Constitution's fulfillment of the purposes of the Declaration: "The *Union*, and the *Constitution*, are the *picture* of *silver*, subsequently framed around it. The picture was made, not to *conceal*, or *destroy* the apple; but to *adorn*, and *preserve* it. The *picture* was made *for* the apple—*not* the apple for the picture." The Declaration states, "That to secure these rights, governments are instituted among men." Thus, Lincoln saw America's union and the Constitution as the setting or "picture of silver" created to secure the rights—the "apple of gold"—that all men and women possessed by nature. However, some Americans had lost sight of this. Having postponed the aboli-tion of black slavery for so long, some had come to believe that liberty belonged only to white people. This confusion over the purpose of the Constitution and the benefit of the American union led to the electoral crisis of 1860.[6]

Lincoln brought his meditation to a close: "So let us act, that neither *picture*, or *apple* shall ever be blurred, or bruised or broken."[7] Here he addressed two distinct misinterpretations of the Constitu-tion that the nation confronted in that critical election year. First there was Stephen Douglas's policy of popular sovereignty. Douglas argued that the enslavement of black people should be decided by the local white populations of states or territories, not by Congress, and steadfastly maintained a neutral stance toward the morality of slav-ery. Lincoln thought this understanding of the federal government divorced the Constitution from the Declaration of Independence. It left the "picture of silver" without an apple, or at least it blurred the apple of gold by viewing the Constitution simply as a mechanism for uniting diverse American states but without a common devotion to human liberty. To Douglas, the *summum bonum* of America was not the equal rights of the individual—"Liberty to all"—but merely the local expression of the people's will regardless of what that will intended, especially with regard to those Douglas deemed "inferior races." Lincoln thought this would "blur" or muddle whatever was framed and to some extent "bruise" any "apple" or political end it intended to adorn by teaching Americans that it did not matter what they willed as long as it reflected the interest of the majority. The consent principle of the Declaration—which Douglas called "a sacred right of suffrage" and "that great principle of self-government"—was thereby neutered as a moral expression of the liberty belonging to each individual.[8] As president-elect, Lincoln explained to the chair-man of the Indiana Republican Party, "I am sorry any republican inclines to dally with Pop. Sov. of any sort. It acknowledges that slavery has equal rights with liberty, and surrenders all we have con-tended for."[9] As long as any American believed that slavery could be a legitimate object of self-government, Lincoln thought genuine majority rule had been subverted.

Lincoln's fame in the mid to late 1850s owed almost entirely to his provoking a public quarrel with U.S. senator Stephen A. Douglas over the proper interpretation of the founders. Douglas took the challenge seriously. During their debates in 1858, he countered Lincoln's claim to understand the founders better than Douglas did. After defeating Lincoln for the Senate, he published an essay in *Harper's New Monthly Magazine* in September 1859 titled "The Dividing Line between Federal and Local Authority: Popular Sovereignty in the Territories." It argued that no power to exercise legislation "in any case whatsoever, is conferred on Congress in respect to the municipal affairs and internal polity, either of the States or of the Territories." Because slavery was a state institution, Douglas believed Congress had no authority over it in the territories. Popular sovereignty should be exercised locally, and therefore the legality of slavery should be determined by the people of a given territory or state.[10]

By 1859, Lincoln made no secret of considering Douglas "the most dangerous enemy of liberty, because the most insidious one." The insidious aspect of Douglas's rhetoric owed to his repeated claim of indifference toward the spread of slavery, by which he meant the enslavement of black people. After Douglas succeeded in passing the Kansas-Nebraska Act of 1854, which repealed the ban on slavery from federal territory declared free as part of the Missouri Compromise of 1820, Lincoln was incensed enough to jump back into politics. As he stated in an 1860 campaign autobiography, "In 1854, his [law] profession had almost superseded the thought of politics in his mind, when the repeal of the Missouri compromise aroused him as he had never been before." In 1854, Lincoln criticized the neutrality of popular sovereignty at the heart of the Kansas-Nebraska Act in no uncertain terms: "This *declared* indifference, but as I must think, covert *real* zeal for the spread of slavery, I can not but hate. I hate it because of the monstrous injustice of slavery itself." His disgust with Douglas's indifference toward slavery was not simply because slavery was obviously wrong, but also because its expansion would not require a positive argument. Simply persuade white Northerners not to care what happens to black people in the federal territories, and slavery would spread as far as self-interest could carry it.[11]

Lincoln therefore argued that the most urgent need was not to refute Southern slave owners but to thwart Douglas's efforts to get Northern non–slave owners to become indifferent to the potential enslavement of black people in the federal territories. "I said that this insidious Douglas popular sovereignty is the measure that now threatens the purpose of the Republican Party, to prevent slavery from being nationalized in the United States." Lincoln thought that Douglas's bowdlerization of true popular sovereignty needed to be the chief target of the Republican Party; otherwise, a "congressional slave code, for the territories, and the revival of the African trade and a second Dred Scott decision" were soon to follow. Lincoln showed that if the North accepted Douglas's popular sovereignty, it would not be long before politicians argued for the repeal of the ban on the importation of slaves, there being no principled difference between allowing slavery to enter federal territory and permitting their purchase where they could be had the cheapest—overseas, which would require only the reintroduction of the international slave trade. Lincoln called attention to this corrupting influence of Douglas's rhetoric, "this gradual and steady debauching of public opinion," what he would later refer to as "the plausible sugar-coated name of which is 'popular sovereignty.'"[12]

The second misinterpretation of the Constitution, Lincoln's "picture" or frame of silver, was the Southern claim that Congress could not ban slavery from the federal territories. Bolstered by the 1857 *Dred Scott* ruling, which agreed with their interpretation, Southerners expected Congress to protect slavery in the territories—a law even Stephen Douglas refused to endorse, which led to the split of the Democratic Party in the summer of 1860. With Lincoln's election that fall and increased Republican representation in the House and Senate, Southerners gave up hope that the federal government would protect "the rights of persons and property in the Territories, and wherever else its Constitutional authority extends." Following the lead of South Carolina, they would now act on their threat to break up the union and form a separate nation.[13]

In his note, Lincoln hoped "that neither *picture*, or *apple* shall ever be . . . broken." By this he meant actions like South Carolina's "to dissolve the union between the State of South Carolina and other states united with her under the compact entitled, 'The Constitution of the United States of America.'" The state's December 20, 1860, secession ordinance repealed its original ratification of the Constitution and declared that its union with the other American states was "hereby dissolved." As Lincoln saw it, South Carolina had broken the "picture of silver." By misconstruing the Constitution as a proslavery document, owing to its original compromises with slavery, the state attempted to secede when it anticipated that Lincoln would not protect slavery. Moreover, this misinterpretation saw the Constitution as a "compact between the States" in their sovereign capacity, as opposed to a compact formed by the people of the United States in their sovereign capacity. South Carolina thought individual states could leave the Union peacefully if the Constitution no longer served the purposes for which they thought it was established. Lincoln, on the other hand, believed the Constitution was a real system of government, not a mere compact or league of sovereign states, and thought that only by becoming this "more perfect union" did self-government have a chance to thrive amid the American states.[14]

He also took seriously the prudence of the founders in dealing with slavery as a preexisting institution in the American states. Lincoln pointed out that the founders did not introduce slavery into the American nation, but rather "found the institution existing among us, which they could not help; and they cast blame upon the British King for having permitted its introduction."[15] Thomas Jefferson's original draft of the Declaration of Independence condemned King George III for "prostitut[ing] his negative for suppressing every legislative attempt to prohibit or to restrain this execrable commerce determining to keep open a market where MEN should be bought & sold." That is, the king sold off his veto power by rejecting colonial attempts to ban the importation of slaves into the American colonies. The paragraph condemning the king for permitting the transatlantic slave trade was deleted by the Second Continental Congress, Jefferson explained, because South Carolina and Georgia had not tried to ban slave importation and because some "Northern brethren . . . had been pretty considerable carriers of them to others."[16] Therefore, the question was how best to deal with slavery's existence in the states as the founders attempted to establish a union of those states dedicated to protecting rights but doing so by the consent of a people not all of whom were ready to give up slavery right away.

When asked to attend a Fourth of July celebration at the Illinois state capital in 1858, Lincoln declined because of an already busy campaign schedule. Nevertheless, he sent along an exhortation to be read to the gathering: "Ever true to *Liberty*, the *Union*, and the Constitution—true to Liberty, not *selfishly*, but upon *principle*—not for special *classes* of men, but for *all* men; true to the Union and the Constitution, as the best means to advance that liberty." Lincoln expected his brief message to be well received because the audience, the German Republicans of the Seventh Ward of Springfield, represented a portion of the Illinois population that had experienced prejudice because of nativist sentiment. He made clear that the American union and the Constitution existed to promote the liberty of the American people.[17]

Lincoln identified allegiance to the Constitution as allegiance to liberty. However, he never identified himself as an abolitionist because of the abolitionists' disdain for the Constitution due to its compromises with slavery. Abolitionists took particular umbrage at its requirement that fugitive slaves be returned to their masters. The most radical wing of abolitionism, led by William Lloyd Garrison, refused to work within the Constitution's federal constraints because it required that abolitionists support a union of free and slave states. Garrison's scorn for the Constitution was manifest. Before the Civil War, the masthead of his newspaper, the *Liberator*, included the statement "NO UNION WITH SLAVEHOLDERS." In 1832, he called the Constitution "the most bloody and heaven-daring arrangement ever made by men" and "an unblushing and monstrous coalition to do evil that good might come." In 1838, he helped establish the Non-Resistance Society, which proclaimed, "We cannot acknowledge allegiance to any human government." In 1845, of "the American Union" he said, "It was conceived in sin, and brought forth in iniquity." In his most infamous formulation, Garrison called the Constitution a "covenant with death," an "agreement with hell," and "a refuge of lies" and concluded that it was "a mighty obstacle in the way of universal freedom and equality." Last, on July 4, 1854, he publicly burned a copy of the Constitution as a concluding act of defiance to federal actions such as the 1850 Fugitive Slave Act. As a pacifist, Garrison sought to motivate fellow citizens to righteous action using only moral suasion, not force, whether by coercion of law or direct violence. "You must perform your duty," he declared, "faithfully, fearlessly and promptly, and leave the consequences to God." Beholden only to his conscience, he gave short shrift to the consent of the governed, which makes government legitimate and, in America's case, brought a union of American states into being and put the mechanisms of self-government into operation.[18]

Lincoln therefore avoided the extremes of both the abolitionism of William Lloyd Garrison and the popular sovereignty of Stephen Douglas. Garrison sought equality for all but could not care less about the consent of the governed. Douglas enshrined majority rule but at the expense of human equality. Lincoln believed justice required both and therefore reminded Americans about the connection between the principles of the Declaration of Independence and the mechanisms of the Constitution and union.

The abolitionists' refusal to uphold all of the Constitution's provisions led Lincoln in 1859 to counsel, to no avail, Governor Salmon P. Chase to persuade Ohio Republicans to stop calling for a repeal of the Fugitive Slave Act: "I assure you the cause of Republicanism is hopeless in Illinois, if it be in any way made responsible for that plank." In a letter that year to Indiana representative Schuyler Colfax, he argued that "tilting against the Fugitive Slave Law" would "utterly overwhelm us in Illinois with the charge of enmity to the constitution itself." He thought the best chances for a national Republican victory in 1860 would be squandered if the relatively new party did not appear to uphold the entire Constitution.[19]

So Lincoln pleaded with fellow Republicans to do nothing that would split the party as it grew in popularity in the North leading up to the pivotal 1860 presidential election. As he wrote almost a year before Republicans held their national convention, "What is desirable, if possible, is that in every local convocation of Republicans, a point should be made to avoid everything which will distract republicans elsewhere." When asked in 1858 by Stephen Douglas whether he supported "the unconditional repeal of the fugitive slave law," Lincoln replied that "under the Constitution of the United States, the people of the Southern States are entitled to a Congressional Fugitive Slave law." Nevertheless, he thought "it should have been framed so as to be free from some of the objections that pertain to it, without lessening its efficiency." The objections had real merit, as they dealt with the rights of due process for the alleged fugitive slave, as well as those compelled to join a posse if needed to apprehend an escaped slave. However, Lincoln thought criticism of the Fugitive Slave Act branded the Republicans as fanatics, thereby dooming their prospects as a national party. He typically kept his reservations to himself, therefore, and focused public attention on preventing slavery from entering the federal territories.[20]

Lincoln wanted all Republicans and former Whigs—in fact, all prospective voters—to be assured about the new party's commitment to uphold all of the Constitution. Lincoln judged that in 1858, this required being explicit about enforcing the Fugitive Slave Act. To be unclear on this point was to bolster Douglas's claim during their 1858 debates that Republicans were no different from abolitionists. Douglas had made repeated reference to Lincoln's party as the "Black Republican party" in hopes that fanatical abolitionism—and with it, doubts about their fidelity to the Constitution—would taint the Republicans.[21] This meant that despite their criticisms of the Fugitive Slave Act, Republicans ought not to make a revision or repeal of the law a leading priority as the party sought to gain its sea legs in the turbulent 1850s.

A major tenet of Lincoln's constitutionalism was his long-standing support for the rule of law. He saw in the rule of law an institutional expression of the prudence and moderation necessary for the perpetuation of self-government. In an effort to thwart the use of mobs to secure swift justice, Lincoln exhorted citizens in 1838 to commit themselves "to the support of the Constitution and the Laws," which he hoped would become "the *political religion* of the nation." This "reverence for the laws" was essential for a free people to maintain their self-governing way of life. To permit outraged citizens to take justice into their own hands because they felt the laws and courts were too slow and cumbersome would lead, Lincoln insisted, to a slippery slope where, "step by step, . . . all the walls erected for the defence of the persons and property of individuals, are trodden down, and disregarded."[22] To act contrarily to the deliberate will of the people by disobeying a law, even in an effort to secure justice, would undermine the stability and security that laws in general provide the community.

Lincoln believed that a vital expression of the rule of law was a strict adherence to federalism, the respect each state owed to the others as part of forming "a more perfect union." Although he spoke more of the union of the states than of federalism per se, union represented the federalism that left most governmental authority at the state and local levels. In discussing the possible annexation of Texas in 1845, Lincoln wrote, "I hold it to be a paramount duty of us in the free states, due to the Union of the states, and perhaps to liberty itself (paradox though it may seem) to let the slavery of the other states alone." However, he added, "I hold it to be equally clear, that we should never knowingly lend ourselves directly or indirectly, to prevent that slavery from dying a natural death—to find new places for it to live in, when it can no longer exist in the old." Lincoln acknowledged the seeming "paradox" of permitting slavery to continue to exist in American states, but he thought that federalism obliged each state to respect the consent operating exclusively within the other states.[23]

After his election to the presidency in 1860, Lincoln affirmed the federal system of American government in a letter quoting the Republican platform, stating that "the maintainance inviolate of the rights of the States, and especially the right of each state to order and control its own domestic institutions according to its own judgment exclusively, is essential to that balance of powers on which the perfection, and endurance of our political fabric depends." His Republican overture to states' rights was intended to set the South at ease regarding the party's intentions about slavery in the states. In his 1858 debates with Douglas, Lincoln said, "We have no power as citizens of the free States or in our federal capacity as members of the Federal Union through the general government, to disturb slavery in the States where it exists." Instead of "warring upon the rights of the States" regarding slavery, Lincoln reiterated the Republican policy "that the new Territories shall be kept free from it while in the Territorial condition." Lincoln explained in his 1861 Message to Congress in Special Session that the American union, and not each state separately, "procured their independence, and their liberty. By conquest, or purchase, the Union gave each of them, whatever of independence, and liberty, it has." He concluded, "The Union is older than any of the States; and, in fact, it created them as States." Without the union, which preceded and established American independence, there would be no individual American states. They would have remained British colonies and under British authority. Their status as independent, self-governing states owed entirely to their acting in concert with the other American colonies to establish their independence and freedom. That said, Lincoln maintained the authority of each state regarding its own domestic policies, including slavery, and was willing to give them their political due as constituent members of the United States of America.[24]

As president, Lincoln took seriously the constitutional limitations regarding abolition. In fact, he opened his First Inaugural Address by declaring that he had "no purpose, directly or indirectly, to interfere with the institution of slavery in the States where it exists" and added that he had "no lawful right to do so" and "no inclination to do so." When pressed to abolish slavery after the war began, he tried to keep the preservation of self-government as the moral justification for the loyal war effort: "We already have an important principle to rally and unite the people in the fact that constitutional government is at stake. This is a fundamental idea, going down about as deep as any thing." A little over a year into the war, as Lincoln prepared to issue an emancipation proclamation, he insisted that Unionists hold fast to their original reason for fighting: to put down a rebellion premised on the fallacious notion that citizens could peacefully disregard an election. Lincoln hoped Americans would see that defending their self-governing way of life was a sufficient war rationale, and one that would motivate them to defend the Union before Lincoln resorted to emancipating slaves as a means of preserving the union.[25]

His most famous statement about the limitations on the federal government's power to abolish slavery took the form of a public letter to *New York Tribune* editor Horace Greeley, who had published an August 1862 editorial lambasting the president for not doing more to enforce Congress's Confiscation Acts. In answer to Greeley, whom Lincoln had gotten to know when they both served in Congress in the late 1840s, he emphasized that he "would save the Union" and "save it the shortest way under the Constitution." After stating this uncontroversial duty of the president, Lincoln turned to the controversial issue of freeing slaves: "If I could save the Union without freeing *any* slave I would do it, and if I could save it by freeing *all* the slaves I would do it; and if I could save it by freeing some and leaving others alone I would also do that." Unknown to Greeley, Lincoln had already drafted a preliminary emancipation proclamation but awaited a Union military victory to show he could enforce it. Here he told Greeley and the American people that only by turning a humanitarian end into a constitutional means could a president employ the executive power to emancipate slaves.[26]

But Lincoln took the opportunity of his public reply to Greeley to distinguish his authority as president from his desire as a fellow human being: "I have here stated my purpose according to my view of *official* duty; and I intend no modification of my oft-expressed *personal* wish that all men every where could be free." He understood that his constitutional authority was a delegated authority, the product of the consent of the American people, and therefore could be exercised only if constitutionally justified. Lincoln repeated this distinction between personal moral convictions and government authority at an 1864 meeting with a Kentucky delegation: "I am naturally anti-slavery. If slavery is not wrong, nothing is wrong. I can not remember when I did not so think, and feel." After stating his personal opposition to slavery, he then pointed out that the Constitution limited his executive authority to address the problem of slavery: "And yet I have never understood that the Presidency conferred upon me an unrestricted right to act officially upon this judgment and feeling." He added that he did not believe that "in ordinary civil administration," his presidential oath—"to preserve the constitution to the best of my ability"—permitted him "to practically indulge [his] primary abstract judgment on the moral question of slavery." Lincoln turned to "military emancipation" only after he had exhausted other means of promoting emancipation by the states themselves. Only by finding constitutional means to achieve constitutional ends did he issue what he later called "the central act of my administration, and the great event of the nineteenth century."[27]

Lincoln's respect for the limitations of the Constitution regarding emancipation derived from his reluctance to amend what he considered a monumental achievement in political prudence by the founders. While in Congress, Lincoln commented briefly on the inadvisability of amending the Constitution. President James Polk had vetoed a bill that included funding for internal improvements in various states, finding no congressional authority in the Constitution to fund said improvements. If the American people wanted Congress to have this authority, they would have to amend the Constitution to accomplish that end.[28] As a good Whig, Lincoln thought the Constitution did empower Congress to fund internal improvements. But on the question of amending the Constitution, he observed, "As a general rule, I think, we would [do] much better [to] let it alone. No slight occasion should tempt us to touch it. Better not take the first step, which may lead to a habit of altering it." Lincoln thought altering the fundamental basis of government would be worse than considering the Constitution unalterable. On balance, a people submissive to the fundamental rule of law would benefit more from a stable government than from a frequent reminder and exercise of their authority to change the basis of their self-government. He added that the Constitution "can scarcely be made better than it is. New provisions, would introduce new difficulties, and thus create, and increase appetite for still further change. . . . The men who made it, have done their work, and have passed away. Who shall improve, on what *they* did?" The more a constitution is amended, the less respect the people will have for it, he believed, as "the supreme law of the land" comes to be seen as just another law, which can be changed as often as the public mood changes.[29]

As president-elect, Lincoln fended off pressure from both political friends and enemies who desired some concession be made to the electoral losers, including the consideration of "an amendment to the constitution which will arrest the progress of secession." He stated, "I do not desire any amendment of the Constitution," but acknowledged that "questions of such amendment rightfully belong to the American People." On the two occasions he did endorse amending the Constitution, both dealt with slavery. One amendment made explicit what Lincoln believed implicit in the Constitution—namely, that Congress could not ban slavery by legislation where it already existed in the states. This "original Thirteenth Amendment," introduced in the House of Representatives by Ohio representative Thomas Corwin (and seconded in the Senate by William Seward, who would soon become Lincoln's secretary of state), stipulated, "No amendment shall be made to the Constitution which will authorize or give to Congress power to abolish or interfere, within any State, with the domestic institutions thereof, including that of persons held to labor or service by the laws of said State." The crisis Lincoln faced upon his inauguration was so great, given the attempt of citizens of seven states to secede from the Union, that he stated in his inauguration address that "holding such a provision to now be implied constitutional law, I have no objection to its being made express, and irrevocable." Lincoln thought that the amendment did nothing more than affirm his long-standing opinion that Congress did not have authority to ban slavery in the states where it already existed. Brooking no compromise with those who called for secession for fear of Republican attacks on slavery, the new president hoped to alleviate this concern from the upper South by acknowledging the recent congressional passage of the Corwin amendment.[30]

Ironically enough, the second time Lincoln endorsed an amendment to the Constitution, he intended the exact opposite result. Lincoln worked mightily to have Congress amend the Constitution to ban slavery throughout the United States. What became the Thirteenth Amendment was the consummation of Lincoln's wartime Emancipation Proclamation, which applied only to areas of the

American union still under rebellion and left intact any state laws or constitutional provisions for the institution of slavery. Specific slaves would have been freed by Lincoln's war proclamation, but slavery itself had yet to be abolished.

Lincoln called the Thirteenth Amendment "a King's cure for all the evils," saying, "It winds the whole thing up." In this case, amending the Constitution made clear its fundamental aim: as its preamble states, to "secure the blessings of liberty." Lincoln had long believed that slavery was "the great Behemoth of danger" and "the only one thing which ever endangers the Union." The Thirteenth Amendment was not only a "great moral victory" but also, returning to the Constitution's preamble, a way to secure "a more perfect union." As Lincoln put it, "He wished the reunion of all the States perfected and so effected as to remove all causes of disturbance in the future." He believed that "to attain this end it was necessary that the original disturbing cause should, if possible, be rooted out." Amending the Constitution he so long had argued against tinkering with became, during a civil war, the best way to preserve that very Constitution's existence. In this case, amending the Constitution served the end that not amending the Constitution had always intended to serve: the security of individual rights. Emancipation secured the freedom of human beings who never should have been robbed of their natural rights, but it became possible only after a civil war created the conditions for a military emancipation that Lincoln justified "as a fit and necessary war measure for suppressing said rebellion." The culmination of this effort, a constitutional amendment, did not change the purpose of the Constitution but upheld the noblest aim of American self-government.[31]

Lincoln made sure to defend publicly the measures he felt compelled to take in defense of the United States from a "gigantic case of Rebellion." He explained that while he respected the constitutional rights of individuals, a concern and responsibility for the public safety led him to employ "strong measures, which by degrees" were necessary to defend the nation. This included suspending the privilege of the writ of habeas corpus. Even with such a controversial act by an executive branch of the federal government, Lincoln cited the constitutional grounds for his action, which was an appeal to the public mind through speeches and public letters. Regardless of where a majority of Americans stood on the question, but especially in the case of those who disagreed with his action, Lincoln pointed to the standard by which his action should be judged—the U.S. Constitution interpreted in light of an insurgency that aimed to dissolve that very Constitution.[32]

Describing Lincoln as a constitutionalist will surprise critics who believe he bent or broke the Constitution in his efforts to preserve the union. Among the most frequently cited charges of his abuse of executive power are his violation of the freedom of the press by allowing opposition newspaper editors to be jailed, permitting military courts to try civilians far away from any battlefield, and especially his suspending the privilege of the writ of habeas corpus. Lincoln was careful to draw attention to the Constitution he was accused of breaking in his defense of how he proceeded as president to deal with the widespread rebellion of citizens in first seven and ultimately eleven "so-called seceded" states. He wrote, "The attention of the country has been called to the proposition that one who is sworn to 'take care that the laws be faithfully executed' should not himself violate them." Addressing the criticism of the suspension of habeas corpus, Lincoln declared, "It was not believed that any law [i.e., constitutional provision] was violated." On August 6, 1861, before Congress adjourned its thirty-day special session, it retroactively approved all of Lincoln's actions in its absence except for the habeas suspension. Congress would not approve of the president exercising this authority until March 3, 1863. (See chapter 5 for a more detailed examination of Lincoln's suspension of habeas corpus.) Whether his audience was persuaded or not, Lincoln highlighted the standard by which his actions as president should be judged: the text of the Constitution.[33]

Lincoln understood the Constitution as a means to an end, but so important a means that it should not be amended except in rare circumstances—and even then, only to fulfill its ultimate purpose: to "secure the Blessings of Liberty to ourselves and our Posterity." In his lifetime, and under his presidential watch, Congress passed an amendment to the Constitution of his fathers—the Thirteenth

Amendment—when a civil war had produced the emancipation of 3 to 4 million black people. To make sure that the freedmen would be included in America's "government of the people, by the people, for the people" and thereby enjoy "a new birth of freedom," that amendment received Lincoln's endorsement and heartfelt efforts to secure its passage. He did not live to see its ratification, which came in December 1865, but made sure to sign the amendment even though that was not required by the Constitution. His signature was testimony to a Constitution changed for the better and hence in keeping with its preamble's aim "to form a more perfect union." The letter of the fundamental law of the land would now be more consistent with its spirit, "the spirit of seventy-six."[34]

No president before or after Lincoln employed political rhetoric more to remind the nation of the vital connection between the just means and ends of American self-government. Lincoln thought that how Americans sought to protect their rights was as important as their conviction that protecting rights was the purpose of government. He believed the founders saw slavery as a moral wrong, but one they could not eliminate in the short run without jeopardizing the union that was instrumental to their independence. The implications of a federal system of government for securing the equal protection of rights was seen most clearly in the founding compromise with slavery in the Constitution. As the next chapter shows, Lincoln made the best of their constitutional compromises with slavery by frequent reference to the natural rights of all human beings. He hoped that a return to the founders' understanding of slavery as a necessary evil would pave the way to its eventual elimination, for he believed it was required of those already secure in their liberty to follow through on the founders' noblest intentions as expressed in the Declaration of Independence.

LINCOLN AND SLAVERY: AN APPEAL
TO THE FOUNDERS' COMPROMISE

> We had slavery among us, we could not get our constitution
> unless we permitted them to remain in slavery, we could not
> secure the good we did secure if we grasped for more, and hav-
> ing by necessity submitted to that much, it does not destroy
> the principle that is the charter of our liberties. Let that charter
> stand as our standard.
>
> —Abraham Lincoln, Speech at Chicago, Illinois (1858)

This chapter explores how Lincoln appealed to the principles and practices of the founders to deal with the problem of slavery. Lincoln explained that despite the existence of slavery in most of the American colonies-turned-states, the founders had never considered slavery a good thing when discussing matters of state: "You may examine the debates under the [Articles of] Confederation, in the Convention that framed the Constitution and in the first session of Congress and you will not find a single man saying that Slavery is a good thing. They all believed it was an evil." However, because of the federal nature of the American union, the individual states possessed the primary authority over slavery, which led to political practices that tolerated slavery as a necessary evil. In his campaign against Stephen Douglas, Lincoln argued that the Republican Party sought to deal with the problem of slavery as the founders had: "Regarding it an evil, they will not molest it in the States where it exists" because "they will not overlook the constitutional guards which our forefathers have placed around it." Nevertheless, like the founders, Republicans intended to "use every constitutional method to prevent the evil from becoming larger" and "restore the government to the policy of the fathers." The U.S. Constitution, which replaced the Articles of Confederation and Perpetual Union, contained restrictions on the powers of the national government as they pertained to internal or domestic institutions, such as slavery. These constitutional compromises with the existence of slavery in several states limited how slavery could be dealt with at the national level.[1]

Lincoln thought slavery was the greatest contradiction of self-government, but he did not infer that the founders approved of slavery because they did not abolish it right away. Instead, he believed that despite clear statements by the founders affirming human equality and condemning slavery, it continued in the American republic because of obstacles that the founding generation faced in emancipating their slaves immediately. Lincoln highlighted the ways that the founding generation took steps toward slavery's eventual elimination: by empowering Congress to cut off the importation of slaves and to prevent it from spreading into the federal territories. These short-term measures stamped moral disapproval on the peculiar institution and intended to lead to its abolition, Lincoln believed, "as fast as circumstances should permit."[2]

During his 1858 campaign for the Senate, Lincoln argued for the fundamental wrongness of slavery by alluding to the Book of Genesis. He thought white Illinoisans might be tempted by Stephen Douglas's popular sovereignty. As discussed in chapter 2, Douglas assured the free state of Illinois that local popular sovereignty did not mean white people had to enslave or mistreat black people: "I would extend to the negro, and the Indian, and to all dependent races every right, every privilege, and every immunity consistent with the safety and welfare of the white races." However, he hastened to add that "equality they never should have, either political or social, or in any other respect whatever."[3] Lincoln, who attended Douglas's July 9 "Homecoming" Speech in Chicago, called Douglas's argument "the same old serpent that says you work and I eat, you toil and I will enjoy the fruits of it." He explained that there was no difference between a king justifying the enslavement of his people and "men of one race" justifying their enslavement of "men of another race." For Lincoln, "it is all the same old serpent." Gleaning from Genesis 3, he associated slavery with the forbidden fruit, which, through the wiles of the devilish serpent, tempted Adam and Eve to fall from grace. In a free society, the political forbidden fruit was slavery, and he thought that those who enjoyed freedom should not give in to the temptation to abuse their freedom by denying it to others.[4]

This became Lincoln's Golden Rule of self-government. In a note to himself, he defined the essence of democracy: "As I would not be a slave, so I would not be a master." The legitimacy and viability of self-government depended on free citizens not thinking they could be good masters. After all, if they thought no one was good enough to rule them without their consent, why would they think they could be good enough to rule others without their consent? Even a master who intended to do good for his slave, given his legal authority over the slave, would eventually rule the slave not in the slave's interest but his own. Lincoln feared that a shift in public opinion regarding the injustice of slavery would become more widespread, to the detriment of the enslaved, if it became associated with a specific race. As he noted in an 1855 letter, "Now when we have grown fat, and have lost all dread of being slaves ourselves, we have become so greedy to be *masters*" that some white Americans had started calling the equality principle of the Declaration "a self-evident lie" to avoid the reciprocity of human equality.[5] He demonstrated to himself the arbitrary basis of racial slavery by taking its premise to its logical conclusion: "You say A. is white, and B. is black. It is *color*, then; the lighter, having the right to enslave the darker? Take care. By this rule, you are to be slave to the first man you meet, with a fairer skin than your own." Applying the same rule to intelligence and interest, he showed with Euclidean precision how political justifications for slavery were simply rationalizations for self-interest. Carried to their logical conclusion, these rationalizations could justify making slaves of the enslavers themselves.[6]

Lincoln flatly disagreed with the change of mind among white Southerners, who, unlike the founders, argued that slavery was good for both master and slave if the masters were white and the slaves were black. He ridiculed the notion that slavery was "good for some people," observing to himself, "As a *good* thing, slavery is strikingly perculiar, in this, that it is the only good thing which no man ever seeks the good of, *for himself.*" Remarking on the manifest selfishness of slavery, he closed with an indignant flourish: "Nonsense! Wolves devouring lambs, not because it is good for their own greedy maws, but because it [is] good for the lambs!!!" Elsewhere Lincoln proclaimed, "Slavery is founded in the selfishness of man's nature," and added that the "love of justice" stood in "eternal antagonism" toward it. He thought this explained why the possibility of slavery's extension into federal territory convulsed the nation so fiercely in the 1850s.[7]

The most famous defense of American slavery as a "positive good" for both master and slave was uttered during the "gag rule" debate in Congress by South Carolina senator John C. Calhoun. He rejected the founding generation's opinion of slavery as "a necessary evil," asserting that "where two races of different origin, and distinguished by color, and other physical differences, as well as intellectual, are brought together, the relation now existing in the slaveholding States between the two, is, instead of an evil, a good—a positive good." Given this radical shift of opinion among white Southerners regarding slavery, Lincoln lamented, "The plainest print cannot be read through a gold eagle." Even the self-evident truths of the Declaration of Independence became obscured and their application to all human beings questioned, if not altogether denied, with the passage of time and economic exploitation.[8]

Lincoln explained that those who desired freedom for themselves must not deprive it from others: "This is a world of compensations; and he who would be no slave, must consent to have no slave. Those who deny freedom to others, deserve it not for themselves; and, under a just God, can not long retain it."[9] A "just God" alluded to Jefferson's Query XVIII in *Notes on the State of Virginia*: "And can the liberties of a nation be thought secure when we have removed their only firm basis, a conviction in the minds of the people that these liberties are of the gift of God? That they are not to be violated but with his wrath? Indeed I tremble for my country when I reflect that God is just: that his justice cannot sleep for ever." Jefferson went on to raise the possibility of a slave rebellion backed by Providence: "The Almighty has no attribute which can take side with us in such a contest." Remarkably, by "us" he meant white slaveholders like himself, who, by prolonging the unjust enslavement of fellow human beings, could not only provoke a race war but provoke one made "probable by supernatural interference!" Like Jefferson, Lincoln invoked a watchful deity over the affairs of the American people, suggesting that freedom would prevail in the long run only if freedom were secured for all inhabitants on American soil.[10]

Lincoln consistently connected the reciprocal nature of human freedom to the security of self-rule. This reciprocity or "world of compensations" dictated that liberties rightly exercised imposed a restraint on those who sought the security of their own liberties. To be secure in one's own freedom, one must not deny someone else his freedom. Lincoln made this point when contrasting his view of the implications of the *Dred Scott* ruling with the view of Stephen Douglas, who Lincoln believed saw the case as "a very small matter at most—that it has no practical effect; that at best, or rather, I suppose, at worst, it is but an abstraction." In 1858, Lincoln repeated his criticism that Douglas saw slavery as "an exceedingly little thing—this matter of keeping one-sixth of the population of the whole nation in a state of oppression and tyranny unequalled in the world" and "as something having no moral question in it." Stumping for Ohio Republicans in September 1859, Lincoln continued his opposition to Douglas by highlighting his indifference toward the plight of black slaves: "I suppose the institution of slavery really looks small to him. He is so put up by nature that a lash upon his back would hurt him, but lash upon anybody else's back does not hurt him." He reminded his audience that "there was once in this country a man by the name of Thomas Jefferson, supposed to be a Democrat—a man whose principles and policy are not very prevalent amongst Democrats to-day, it is true; but that man did not take exactly this view of the insignificance of the element of slavery which our friend Judge

Douglas does." Whereas earlier in 1859, Lincoln had only alluded to Jefferson's *Notes on the State of Virginia*, he now directly quoted the sentence expressing Jefferson's fear regarding the continued enslavement of men and women on American soil after the Revolution: "I tremble for my country when I remember that God is just!" Lincoln interpreted Jefferson's statement as a warning to posterity: in Lincoln's words, "danger to this country—danger of the avenging justice of God in that little unimportant popular sovereignty question of Judge Douglas." Lincoln understood Jefferson to have seen "a question of God's eternal justice wrapped up in the enslaving of any race of men, or any man, and that those who did so braved the arm of Jehovah—that when a nation thus dared the Almighty every friend of that nation had cause to dread His wrath." Lincoln challenged his Ohio audience to choose "between Jefferson and Douglas as to what is the true view of this element among us." Douglas called his policy of popular sovereignty "the great principle of self-government," even though it permitted white settlers to enslave black people in federal territory. Lincoln believed that slavery so obviously contradicted "self-government" that to "call it so" was "simply absurd and ridiculous."[11]

How he approached the abolition of slavery owes much to his understanding of how the American founders approached the difficult issue of slavery, an institution that existed long before Americans sought independence from England on the basis of human equality and government by consent of the governed. Time and again, Lincoln's references to the founders centered on how they tried to establish a government based on human equality. But adherence to that very principle imposed on them the requirement that slavery be abolished in a manner consistent with the consent that was the only legitimate grounds for self-government. Simply put, consent was the flip side of the equality coin, and that very consent limited the means by which slavery could be eliminated.

Abolitionists agreed with Lincoln and the founders that slavery was a moral evil but went on to demand that if the slave states did not emancipate their slaves immediately (and without compensation), then the federal government should step in to do so. Some abolitionists expressed their opinions with extreme language and condemnatory rhetoric that exacerbated the public divide over slavery. In 1837, Lincoln joined only one other Illinois state representative, Dan Stone, in declaring that "the institution of slavery is founded on both injustice and bad policy; but that the promulgation of abolition doctrines tends rather to increase than to abate its evils." Lincoln believed the abolitionists were their own worst enemies in using inflammatory rhetoric that stiffened the resolve of Southern slave owners and therefore undermined their efforts to abolish slavery. By refusing to concede that the federal Constitution did not permit states to dictate to each other what to do regarding their own "domestic institutions," which included slavery, and by calling for the repeal of the 1850 Fugitive Slave Act, abolitionists found few political friends to join their fight against slavery. Lincoln would always maintain his opposition to slavery but never counted himself among the abolitionists precisely for these reasons.[12]

Lincoln's insistence that Congress prevent slavery from entering the territories did not mean that he forgot the restraints of the Constitution on federal antislavery measures. He believed that Northerners, in fact, showed exemplary moderation in respecting the legal rights of Southern slave owners. In 1855, he wrote to his closest friend and former business partner, Joshua Speed, who had moved back to Kentucky from Illinois, conveying his frustration that slave owners like Speed failed to "appreciate how much the great body of the Northern people do crucify their feelings, in order to maintain their loyalty to the constitution and the Union." Lincoln insisted, "I . . . acknowledge *your* rights and *my* obligations, under the constitution, in regard to your slaves," but wanted Speed to know, "I hate to see the poor creatures hunted down, and caught, and carried back to their stripes, and unrewarded toils; but I bite my lip and keep quiet." This illustrated how American federalism prevented the national abolition of slavery by Congress. But it also showed the lengths to which antislavery opinion in the free states submitted its fondest hopes for emancipation to the constraints of a political union that limited the power of the nation as a whole to abolish slavery.[13]

Lincoln closed his letter by responding to Speed's query about his partisan affiliation. With the Whig Party on the wane since its dismal showing in the 1852 election, he explained that he was "not a Know-Nothing" precisely because of his devotion to the Declaration of Independence. Given his reading of it to include black people, Lincoln could not identify as a Know-Nothing because of the party's anti-Catholic, anti-immigrant policies. Know-Nothings read the Declaration as an exclusive charter of liberty, which led to a slippery slope that excluded not only black people but also groups of white people. For the equality principle to be a solid basis for self-government, it must be universal: it must apply to all human beings. Otherwise, exceptions could be made by whatever majority happened to hold power. "When it comes to this," Lincoln concluded, "I should prefer emigrating to some country where they make no pretence of loving liberty—to Russia, for instance, where despotism can be taken pure, and without the base alloy of hypocracy." He feared this corruption of constitutional self-government, as it would turn popular government into mere majority rule with no respect for the rights of the minority.[14]

Only a week earlier, Lincoln had written to another Kentucky associate, Judge George Robertson, lamenting, "That spirit which desired the peaceful extinction of slavery, has itself become extinct, with the occasion, and the men of the Revolution." That liberating spirit had moved citizens of six of the original thirteen American states to free their slaves. But he noted that "not a single state has done the like since." In his most pessimistic remarks regarding the prospects for emancipation, Lincoln stated that he doubted it would happen peacefully: "Our political problem now is 'Can we, as a nation, continue together permanently—forever—half slave, and half free?' The problem is too mighty for me. May God, in his mercy, superintend the solution." He even compared the state of black American slaves with "the lost souls of the finally impenitent," suggesting with pitiful exaggeration that they were politically doomed. Lincoln then judged his own generation inferior to the slaveholding generation of the fathers: "On the question of liberty, as a principle, we are not what we have been." In Lincoln's mind, the grand irony of America's devotion to liberty was that despite being surrounded by slaves, Americans had been more committed to abolishing slavery during the founding generation than in Lincoln's time, when slavery had become situated almost entirely in the South and the nation's commitment to emancipation appeared to be fading away.[15] In 1857, a Supreme Court ruling confirmed Lincoln's worst fears about the prospects for reclaiming the founders' approach to the slavery question.

When the court ruled that Dred Scott, as a descendant of African slaves, could not sue in federal court and that Congress did not have the authority to ban slavery in the federal territories, Lincoln and the Republican Party were put in a difficult position. The central plank of their 1860 platform was the belief in Congress's authority to ban slavery in the territories. They noted that because "our Republican fathers . . . abolished slavery in all our national territory," Americans were duty-bound to "deny the authority of Congress, of a territorial legislature, or of any individuals, to give legal existence to slavery in any territory of the United States." For the highest court in the land to say that Congress violated the Constitution when it banned slavery in the Louisiana Territory north of the 36°30' parallel, the famous Missouri Compromise of 1820, meant the Republican Party no longer had any reason for being. In fact, Stephen Douglas argued that Lincoln's opposition to the court's decision was an act of "warfare upon the Supreme Court." Lincoln disagreed and maintained that citizens could take issue with the actions of their government and pursue peaceful, political remedies to get the government to change its mind.[16]

Lincoln's fidelity to the U.S. Constitution required him to leave slavery alone where it already existed but keep it from expanding into federal territory. Over time, states where slavery was legal would find a way to wean themselves off of "the peculiar institution" and eliminate slavery gradually and peacefully. The federal nature of the national government prevented it from abolishing slavery, which was considered a local institution and therefore could be regulated only by state government. At the founding, the American people vested Congress with legislative authority only over interstate matters or the states collectively as they related to the Indian tribes and foreign nations. Congress could address slavery only in matters relating to the states as a whole or in relation to foreign governments. Thus, it could and did ban the importation of slaves because that involved trade with foreign nations. Following the precedent of the Congress under the Articles of Confederation and Perpetual Union, Congress under the U.S. Constitution also chose to ban slavery in the Northwest Territory. Tracing these early actions of the national government, Lincoln argued that by stopping slavery at its source while also preventing its spread into the western territories, the American citizenry—at least in the early days of the Republic—put slavery on the course of ultimate extinction.

Lincoln made a useful distinction between being antislavery and being abolitionist, two terms that in the twenty-first century appear synonymous. In Lincoln's day, abolitionists were considered a fringe element of society, even extremists or fanatics, chiefly because of their uncompromising commitment to equality. In some cases, their devotion to equality came at the expense of the Constitution and rule of law, which fundamentally provided the means of securing one's rights. Most famously, William Lloyd Garrison, editor of the newspaper the *Liberator* and among the preeminent spokesmen of abolitionists, burned a copy of the Constitution publicly, emblazoned his newspaper with the motto "NO UNION WITH SLAVEHOLDERS," and spoke with fiery rhetoric to stir Northerners from their apathy. In contrast, Lincoln believed in human equality no less than Garrison: "I have always hated slavery, I think as much as any Abolitionist." However, he thought not only that prudence should play a role in eradicating slavery but also that the compromises with slavery that produced the federal Constitution needed to be upheld for the sake of peace among the American states.[17]

Lincoln distinguished between abolishing slavery where it already existed and preventing the spread of slavery into areas where it did not exist. Lincoln sought to establish the latter policy as the best way to begin the eventual eradication of slavery from the United States. In 1859, looking ahead to the national elections in 1860, Lincoln exhorted fellow Republicans to avoid "divisions in the Republican ranks." Given the steady hue and cry over the status of the federal Fugitive Slave Act of 1850, he counseled Republicans in various states to "forbear tilting against the Fugitive Slave law." This would harm their efforts in other states, where opponents would use their opposition to the law to claim Republican animosity toward the Constitution, which stipulated that fugitive slaves be returned to their legal masters. Thus, as he considered "the spread and nationalization of slavery . . . a national concern," which "must be attended to by the nation," Lincoln tried to keep the party's focus on the threat of slavery's expansion into the federal territories. Their policy should be to put slavery "back upon the basis where our fathers placed it," as he noted in his 1858 debates with Stephen Douglas, which meant "keep[ing] it out of our new Territories—to restrict it forever to the old States where it now exists." Only then would "the public mind . . . rest in the belief that it is in the course of ultimate extinction."[18]

As explored in chapter 3, Lincoln never referred to himself as an abolitionist, but he was emphatic in his antislavery statements, which he thought expressed his commitment to abolishing slavery in a manner consistent with the federal Constitution. Lincoln made clear in 1859 that Americans needed to retain the founders' conviction that slavery was wrong in principle but tolerated because of the compromise necessary to maintain the union of the American states: "It is no just function of government to prohibit what is *not wrong*." Lincoln added, "In short, there is no justification for prohibiting slavery anywhere, save only in the assumption that slavery is wrong. And whenever the sentiment, that slavery is *wrong*, shall give way in the North, all legal prohibitions of it will also give way." Lincoln explained that in the most fundamental sense, government exists to secure justice, which is another way of saying to prevent injustice. For him, and most Northerners, slavery was wrong, and therefore government should not extend an institution that preexisted the formation of the American union but, because of the federal nature of their national government, had been compromised with to secure "a more perfect union."[19]

More to his point, Lincoln showed the connection between what people believe to be wrong and what government ought not to permit. Laws can do their job only as well as the public opinion that supports them. Northern states had banned slavery, but if their opinion regarding slavery changed to outright approval or even mere indifference,

Lincoln argued, the laws would soon reflect this change. He presented this argument not only to keep free states free but also to indicate how freedom would eventually come to slave states. It would begin with a conviction among slave state citizens that slavery was a moral evil. Eventually their laws and constitutions would change to reflect that sentiment. That was how Lincoln thought the peculiar institution could be eradicated in America in a peaceful way.

On July 9, 1858, Lincoln attended a speech by Stephen Douglas, who had returned to Chicago at the adjournment of Congress. A month earlier, Lincoln was chosen unanimously by the Illinois Republican Party to challenge Douglas for his Senate seat, and Douglas took the opportunity to respond to Lincoln's criticisms. The following day, Lincoln responded to Douglas's speech and drew attention to their opposing interpretations of the founders' intentions regarding the future of slavery in the United States. He insisted that "the opponents of slavery" meant only to "resist the farther spread of it, and place it where the public mind shall rest with the belief that it is in course of ultimate extinction." In so doing, they would thereby "place it where the founders of this Government originally placed it." Ever since Lincoln returned to the political arena in 1854, he made a habit of highlighting the founders' approach toward the problem of slavery. It was a necessary evil they did not know how to get rid of immediately, but the federal system of government equipped Americans to eliminate it gradually and peacefully over time as slave states came around to ridding themselves of the peculiar institution.[20]

Lincoln pointed out the ways that the Constitution, although it did not empower Congress to ban slavery where it already existed, did grant the federal government authority to treat slavery as an evil by preventing continued importation into the nation and its federal territory: "Why did those old men, about the time of the adoption of the Constitution, decree that Slavery should not go into the new Territory, where it had not already gone? Why declare that within twenty years the African Slave Trade, by which slaves are supplied, might be cut off by Congress?" Lincoln concluded that these actions were "a clear indication that the framers of the Constitution intended and expected the ultimate extinction of that institution." What would otherwise be interpreted as mere compromises with slavery by the young republic should be viewed instead, Lincoln argued, as signs of their disapproval of the institution and an interest in its removal as soon as practicable.[21]

A week later, he elaborated on the theme by explaining how the founders could disapprove of slavery but not eliminate it right away. He pointed out, "When our Government was established, we had the institution of slavery among us. We were in a certain sense compelled to tolerate its existence." In what sense were the founders forced to allow slavery to survive the formation of the new republic? "It was a sort of necessity. We had gone through our struggle and secured our own independence. The framers of the Constitution found the institution of slavery amongst their other institutions at the time. They found that by an effort to eradicate it, they might lose much of what they had already gained." As Harry Jaffa once put it, "To have asked for more would not have been to gain more but rather to lose everything." Lincoln interpreted the slowness of the founders to eliminate slavery as an indication of the political constraints at a time when they were struggling to form an independent nation out of thirteen former colonies. Liberty was the goal, but it required—by the terms of their own Declaration of Independence—the consent of the members of a political union still in the making. Slavery could not be abolished peacefully, and consistently with the rule of law, until those members found a way to wean themselves off of it.[22]

Here Lincoln helped his generation see the bigger picture, which encompassed constitutional power and legislative action directed toward the removal of slavery: "They gave power to Congress to abolish the slave trade at the end of twenty years. They also prohibited it in the Territories where it did not exist. They did what they could and yielded to the necessity for the rest." A month later, Lincoln raised the question that if "the Fathers of the Republic" had actually thought slavery a boon to their new nation, why did they allow Congress to ban slave importation in twenty years? It was necessary, Lincoln answered, "to *prevent* the people, through Congress, from putting a stop to the traffic *immediately* at the close of the war." There must have been a strong majority sentiment to ban the slave trade in 1787, but a concession was made to a small minority of states—namely, South Carolina and Georgia—to prevent Congress from doing so before 1808.[23]

Contrary to Stephen Douglas's claim that peace would come to the nation by simply leaving the slavery question to each state and territory to do as it saw fit, Lincoln argued in 1858 that peace had prevailed in the country only when the public thought slavery was "in the course of ultimate extinction." In fact, Lincoln added, "I have believed—and now believe—the public mind did rest on that belief up to the introduction of the Nebraska bill" In 1854, Lincoln noticed a trend in the nation, as "the men of the present age, by their experience, have become wiser than the framers of the Constitution; and the invention of the cotton gin had made the perpetuity of slavery a necessity in this country." Nevertheless, as long as men such as Douglas claimed their policies reflected the principles of the founders, Lincoln expected that a more accurate presentation of their principles and practices would lead his generation to return to the founders' approach by treating slavery as an evil to be restricted in hopes that it would wither away over time.[24]

In his seventh and final formal debate with Stephen Douglas, on October 15, 1858, Lincoln made his customary appeal to the founders for guidance on the slavery question. He argued that "the fathers of this Government placed that institution where the public mind *did* rest in the belief that it was in the course of ultimate extinction." They had sought to eliminate slavery not by attacking it in the states where it already existed but by keeping it from spreading into the federal territories. In addition, the framers had even kept the word *slavery* out of the Constitution, intending the Constitution to "endure forever" but expecting slavery "to come to an end." Drawing from James Madison's notes on the Constitutional Convention, Lincoln concluded that "there should be nothing on the face of the great charter of liberty suggesting that such a thing as negro slavery had ever existed among us." Lincoln summed up this approach of the fathers: "You see this peaceful way of dealing with it as a wrong—restricting the spread of it, and not allowing it to go into new countries where it has not already existed. That is the peaceful way, the old-fashioned way, the way in which the fathers themselves set us the example." His insistence that Congress possessed the authority to prevent slavery's extension into federal territory remained the raison d'être of the Republican Party.[25]

Lincoln believed in this so strongly that as president-elect, he rejected entreaties to compromise on the nonextension plank by those hoping to avert secession: "Prevent, as far as possible, any of our friends from demoralizing themselves, and our cause, by entertaining propositions for compromise of any sort, on 'slavery extention.'" He demanded that they "hold firm, as with a chain of steel." The Republicans had campaigned and won elections on that policy in 1860. It was no time to concede the very principle that had given birth to the party in 1854. Back then, Lincoln had argued that during the founding era, "the plain unmistakable spirit of that age, towards slavery, was hostility to the PRINCIPLE, and toleration, ONLY BY NECESSITY." Lincoln believed the Republicans had the founders on their side by insisting on treating slavery as a wrong to be tolerated where necessary but curbed and hampered in hopes of its falling away peacefully over time. Preserving an American union "forever worthy of the saving" required no less.[26]

As Lincoln observed early in 1860, when framing the new federal Constitution, the founders saw "the slave trade existing; capital invested in it; fields depending upon it for labor, and the whole system resting upon the importation of slave-labor. They therefore did not prohibit the slave trade at once, but they gave the power to prohibit it after twenty years." The international slave trade was the only exception made to Congress's authority to regulate foreign trade under the new Constitution. Lincoln asked, "Would they have done this if they had not thought slavery wrong?" The framers compromised with South Carolina and Georgia by extending for twenty years the right of states to import slaves from abroad. But this was necessary "to form a more perfect union" of the American states. The alternative would have resulted in the dissolution of the United States less than a decade after securing independence from Great Britain, thus jeopardizing the prospects for freedom in North America and any hope of liberation for slaves in the Southern states. The founders believed slavery was wrong in principle, so they took pains both to curb its supply and to keep it from spreading. Prudence dictated that the mechanisms of self-government, reflecting the workings of human frailty, custom, habit, and economic realities, would need time to catch up with the ideals of self-government. Lincoln hoped that by returning to the founders' approach to slavery, restricting its spread as the first step toward its eventual eradication, Republicans could put the nation back on the path to respectable prosperity.[27]

Lincoln's return to the founders on the most vexing problem in the nation's history raises an important question to be answered about his appeal to the founding: why did the birth of America, in its political principles and structures, deserve Lincoln's respect? Why did its introduction of a *novus ordo seclorum*, "a new order of the ages," strike Lincoln as the most relevant guide for the problems of his own era? The next chapter will consider the value Lincoln found in looking to America's past and his counsel regarding when that past should be disregarded in place of new and better ways for Americans to rule themselves.[28]

LINCOLN AND ORIGINAL INTENT: AN APPEAL TO THE FOUNDERS' RELEVANCE

If we would supplant the opinions and policy of our fathers in any case, we should do so upon evidence so conclusive, and argument so clear, that even their great authority, fairly considered and weighed, cannot stand.

—Abraham Lincoln, Address at Cooper Institute (1860)

This chapter explores the concept of original intent by considering how Lincoln understood his own reverence for the American founding in light of the responsibility of succeeding generations to govern themselves according to their own understanding of what their times required. Respect for their original intentions is important not simply because they came first. After all, not all old things are worth preserving. That said, an old nation or government should not be rejected simply because it is old. Nevertheless, Lincoln argued that preserving what is old, even a form of government, should find its justification most importantly in the merits: to wit, each generation of Americans should follow those intentions and practices of their forebears that are worthy of their respect, which is to say, because they are right. It stands to reason that what is no longer understood to be true in principle or useful in practice should be replaced by something better.

Lincoln discussed original intention most directly in his 1860 Cooper Institute Address. He raised the subject at the beginning of the speech as he set out to refute Stephen Douglas's claim to be following the policy of the founders, especially regarding the federal government's authority to regulate slavery in the federal territories. Douglas thought the founders did not intend for Congress to exercise this authority but instead allowed local popular sovereignty to regulate domestic institutions like slavery. He made the case in speeches, such as one in Columbus, Ohio, on September 7, 1859, and in an article published that same month in *Harper's New Monthly Magazine*.[1] Lincoln was glad to see Douglas affirm the authority of the framers of the Constitution. After quoting Douglas's 1859 speech, where Douglas stated, "Our fathers, when they framed the Government under which we live, understood this question just as well, and even better, than we do now," Lincoln replied, "I fully indorse this, and I adopt it as a text for this discourse." This framed their disagreement as a debate over the correct interpretation of the "fathers." They both agreed that the founders should be followed by subsequent generations of Americans; they disagreed about what the founders intended. Because Lincoln also understood that not everything old was worthy of respect, he therefore raised the question of when, if ever, the intentions of the "fathers" should be rejected.[2]

Lincoln devoted the opening third of his Cooper Institute speech to refuting Douglas's claims regarding the framers of the Constitution. As Lincoln concluded this opening section of his speech, he explained that his devotion to the founders was no blind fealty: "I do not mean to say we are bound to follow implicitly in whatever our fathers did. To do so, would be to discard all the lights of current experience—to reject all progress—all improvement." In that pivotal campaign year of 1860, Lincoln argued that Americans should not follow what was old, even the founders of their country, if experience showed they could improve on their long-standing belief and practice. "What I do say is," Lincoln continued, "that if we would supplant the opinions and policy of our fathers in any case, we should do so upon evidence so conclusive, and argument so clear, that even their great authority, fairly considered and weighed, cannot stand."

Lincoln hastened to add that he did not see a better way forward for the country, given the debate over the future of slavery, than the mode adopted by the founders. Innovations like Stephen Douglas's crude version of popular sovereignty and the Southern defense of slavery as a "positive good" for both master and slave were clearly deficient when compared with a faithful account of the principles and practices of founders now dead and gone.[3]

The question of innovation or progress versus original intention is an important one, especially given the modern tendency to treat anything new as if it were necessarily improved. Lincoln acknowledged that experience could lead to progress and improvement. Nevertheless, when white Southerners began justifying the enslavement of black people as beneficial for both the master and the enslaved, Lincoln believed their new approach to an old evil was emphatically no improvement. He noticed that "although volume upon volume is written to prove slavery a very good thing, we never hear of the man who wishes to take the good of it, *by being a slave himself.*"[4] He thought the progress of America occurred despite slavery, not because some white people devised ways to justify it as good for all concerned.

Lincoln also believed the rule of law to be an essential way that a free people maintained their liberties over time. This led him to respect the wisdom of his predecessors unless he saw clear room for improvement. For example, when some proposed to amend the Constitution to state explicitly that Congress could fund infrastructure within the states, he argued, "As a general rule, I think, we would much better let it alone. No slight occasion should tempt us to touch it. Better not take the first step, which may lead to a habit of altering it." He thought a tendency to change the fundamental law of the land would give up the benefit of stability in government. Of course, a stable government works best when it is good government. Thus, Lincoln affirmed that the Constitution could "scarcely be made better than it is" and doubted anyone could improve on what the framers had achieved.[5]

That achievement took into account the necessity, as Lincoln saw it, of accommodating slave states such as South Carolina and Georgia to maintain the constitutional union of the states. A clear example of what he would change if it would not disrupt the American union would be the compromises in the Constitution respecting slavery: in particular, the notorious three-fifths compromise regarding slavery and congressional representation, the extradition of fugitive slaves, and the ban against Congress preventing the importation of slaves prior to 1808. But as he said of slavery in the states in 1859, "The peace of society, and the structure of our government both require that we should let it alone, and we insist on letting it alone."[6] This shows how fragile Lincoln believed the union of American states was, and why he preached not only devotion to the Constitution but also adherence to compromises that preserved the union even at the cost of maintaining slavery where it already existed.

Critics of original intention like to mention Chief Justice Roger B. Taney as Exhibit A, given that his opinion in *Dred Scott v. Sanford* is commonly cited as the worst decision the Supreme Court ever handed down.[7] In that case, Taney observed that his job was not to decide the case according to what his generation believed about the status of black people in the United States. Instead, the court should follow the practices of the founding era toward black people. According to Taney, neither the laws of those bygone days nor the words of the Declaration of Independence indicated that free or enslaved black people "were then acknowledged as a part of the people, nor intended to be included in the general words used in that memorable instrument." Taney then turned to the framing of the Constitution "to determine whether the general terms used in the Constitution of the United States as to the rights of man and the rights of the people was intended to include them, or to give to them or their posterity the benefit of any of its provisions." Because he thought that "the state of public opinion" during the founding period was "difficult" for his generation to discern, Taney drew upon "the public history of every European nation" to determine its likely impact on the American colonies regarding the legal status of black people. "They had for more than a century before been regarded as beings of an inferior order," he surmised, "and altogether unfit to associate with the white race either in social or political relations." Then, in the most notorious statement of his ruling, Taney added that black people were "so far inferior that they had no rights which the white man was bound to respect, and that the negro might justly and lawfully be reduced to slavery for his benefit." This view of black people "was naturally impressed upon the colonies" by England, and according to Taney, it became "the prevailing opinion" when the Declaration and Constitution were written.[8]

As proof, Taney cited colonial laws discriminating against black people as evidence of their "degraded condition" in the American colonies. He then cited the most familiar sentence of the Declaration of Independence to demonstrate that its "language" was "equally conclusive": "We hold these truths to be self-evident: that all men are created equal; that they are endowed by their Creator with certain unalienable rights; that among them is life, liberty, and the pursuit of happiness." Taney admitted that the words "would seem to embrace the whole human family, and if they were used in a similar instrument at this day would be so understood." Nevertheless, he did not think they should be interpreted by the court by their meaning in his day because "the conduct of the distinguished men who framed the Declaration of Independence would have been utterly and flagrantly inconsistent with the principles they asserted." What conduct? "The unhappy black race were separated from the white by indelible marks, and laws long before established, and were never thought of or spoken of except as property." In short, because they did not emancipate their slaves immediately upon declaring that "all men are created equal," the founders could not have intended to include black people. Because "the men who framed this declaration were great men—high in literary acquirements, high in their sense of honor," they were "incapable of asserting principles inconsistent with those on which they were acting." Judging the founders' words by their deeds—or lack thereof—Taney concluded that neither the Declaration nor the Constitution applied to black people.[9]

With this reading of the founders' intentions settled in his mind, Taney explained, "No one, we presume, supposes that any change in public opinion or feeling, in relation to this unfortunate race . . . should induce the court to give to the words of the Constitution a more liberal construction in their favor than they were intended to bear when the instrument was framed and adopted." He believed his responsibility as a judge forbade him to interpret and apply the Constitution according to the sentiments of his time. Instead, "while it remains unaltered, it must be construed now as it was understood at the time of its adoption." Thus, Taney argued that the Constitution "speaks not only in the same words, but with the same meaning and intent with which it spoke when it came from the hands of its framers and was voted on and adopted by the people of the United States." To argue otherwise "would abrogate the judicial character of this court, and make it the mere reflex of the popular opinion or passion of the day."[10]

Lincoln had no problem with Taney interpreting the Constitution's words according to "the same meaning and intent" of the constitutional framers and ratifiers; he just did not think Taney did so correctly and without bias. As shown in chapter 2, Lincoln rejected Taney's interpretation of the Declaration, which read the black man out of its universal application. "In those days," Lincoln argued, "our Declaration of Independence was held sacred by all, and thought to include all." He believed the founders understood that all human beings possessed natural rights and that the protection of those rights was based on the consent of the governed. To be sure, white Americans were slow to protect the rights of all black people in the early republic. Taney interpreted that slowness to mean they did not believe in the natural rights of black people. Lincoln thought this reading of the original intention of the founders was mistaken, and he drew from a dissenter in the *Dred Scott* case to mount a rebuttal.[11]

Lincoln agreed with Justice Benjamin Curtis's dissent in the *Dred Scott* case, which directly contradicted Taney's claim that black people formed no part of the people for whom the Declaration or Constitution were written. In fact, he quoted Curtis's dissent to show that during the debates over ratifying the U.S. Constitution, black citizens in at least five states "had the power to act, and, doubtless, did act, by their suffrages, upon the question of its adoption." Taney simply ignored the history presented by Curtis, as it would undermine his claim of universal disfavor toward blacks during the Revolutionary era. Lincoln found Taney's ruling, which "assumed historical facts which were not really true," deficient in several respects. He therefore argued that an "erroneous" decision of the Supreme Court, while "absolutely determin[ing] the case decided" and hence to be obeyed by all, need not be considered "a settled doctrine for the country."[12]

This criticism of the court's decision led Stephen Douglas to lambaste Lincoln and the Republicans for "resisting" the *Dred Scott* ruling. Douglas claimed that "when the decision is made, my private opinion, your opinion, all other opinions must yield to the majesty of that authoritative adjudication." As Lincoln saw it, Douglas was teaching the American people to treat court decisions as a "*Thus saith the Lord*," never to be questioned. This would undermine the ultimate authority that the citizenry had to govern themselves. How should the American people expect the highest court in the land to adjudicate constitutional questions so that they have the force of law without robbing the people of their sovereignty? Lincoln and fellow Republicans aimed to get the court to reverse its decision.[13]

To that end, Lincoln quoted Andrew Jackson, the idol of Stephen Douglas and Northern Democrats, on the limited role of precedent: "Mere precedent is a dangerous source of authority, and should not be regarded as deciding questions of constitutional power, except where the acquiescence of the people and the States can be considered as well settled." He also cited Jackson to support the right of each federal branch of government to interpret the Constitution for itself in the exercise of its respective powers: "The Congress, the executive and the court, must each for itself be guided by its own opinion of the Constitution. Each public officer, who takes an oath to support the Constitution, swears that he will support it as he understands it, and not as it is understood by others." Lincoln reminded his audience that the Supreme Court "has often over-ruled its own decisions, and we shall do what we can to have it to over-rule" the *Dred Scott* decision, but insisted that Republicans "offer no *resistance* to it." This was a long-held view of Lincoln's, stretching back to his tenure as an Illinois state representative. In 1838, he observed that "although bad laws, if they exist, should be repealed as soon as possible, still while they continue in force, for the sake of example, they should be religiously observed." In the case of Supreme Court decision, Lincoln counseled that Republicans would abide by the decision even as they worked through Congress to compel the court to revisit the issue.[14]

He repeated this argument in his First Inaugural Address, contending that if government policies on important questions were "irrevocably fixed by decisions of the Supreme Court, . . . the people will have ceased, to be their own rulers, having, to that extent, practically resigned their government, into the hands of that eminent tribunal." Lincoln maintained that a free people never gave up their ultimate responsibility to rule themselves, even as they obeyed the rulers that governed by their consent. He put the matter bluntly in 1859 when he declared that citizens were "the rightful masters of both Congresses and courts not to overthrow the constitution, but to overthrow the men who pervert that constitution." The real "masters" in America were the citizens, who were responsible to hold their rulers accountable to them and to their understanding of the Constitution.[15]

In the midst of a war to preserve the ideals and institutions of self-government, those citizens eventually sought to amend their Constitution to ensure that slavery would no longer threaten the perpetuation of free government. However, neither Lincoln nor Congress assumed office in 1861 intending to abolish slavery, let alone amend the Constitution. Moreover, as Lincoln observed in his Second Inaugural Address, neither side in the war expected "that the *cause* of the conflict might cease with, or even before, the conflict itself should cease. Each looked for an easier triumph, and a result less fundamental and astounding." However, the vicissitudes of war prompted two confiscation acts by Congress and the Emancipation Proclamation by the president. These, in turn, spurred a movement—eventually supported by Lincoln—to abolish slavery by constitutional amendment. Did this reflect a shift in Lincoln's reverence for the Constitution? Was his endorsement of the Thirteenth Amendment a departure from the original intention of the founders or its fulfillment?[16]

Although Lincoln preferred not to alter the Constitution of the fathers, he lobbied for the Thirteenth Amendment after his reelection in 1864 to ensure that the war's conclusion would also guarantee that slavery would never resurface in any of the states. However, his wartime endorsement of the amendment followed a radical shift in the Southern states away from what he believed was the founders' expectation of slavery's eventual demise. When white Southerners insisted the Constitution must protect slavery in the federal territories, Lincoln had hoped that they would have "too much of good sense, and good temper, to attempt the ruin of the government, rather than see it administered as it was administered by the men who made it." They chose war instead of submitting to a Republican president. Lincoln eventually backed the Thirteenth Amendment to make explicit the original intention of a republic free of slavery. However, he would not have endorsed a constitutional amendment had the rebellion been put down sooner and Congress followed through on the Republican effort to prevent the extension of slavery into federal territory. Lincoln had always preferred that slaveholding states abolish the peculiar institution, just as the Northern states had done in the early days of the republic. As president, he appealed to the loyal slaveholding states during the war to adopt gradual abolition plans to demoralize the rebellious states and speed the war's end. In this scenario, Lincoln would have presided over "the Union as it was," and hence reclaimed the founders' original aspirations for the nation without amending the federal Constitution.[17]

The relevance of this discussion of original intent can be seen in our modern era as debates continue regarding whether "originalism" should inform Supreme Court jurisprudence. This was seen most clearly in the mid-1980s, when Attorney General Edwin Meese III spoke to the American Bar Association. In a speech titled "Jurisprudence of Original Intention," he argued that the Reagan administration would "endeavor to resurrect the original meaning of constitutional provisions and statutes as the only reliable guide for judgment." Meese thought that if the Constitution was simply whatever the Supreme Court said it meant, then it was not serving the purpose of a constitution, which was to prevent popular majorities from infringing upon individual rights. Meese concluded, "It is our belief that only 'the sense in which the Constitution was accepted and ratified by the nation,' and only the sense in which laws were drafted and passed provide a solid foundation for adjudication." For judges to do otherwise "suffers the defect of pouring new meaning into old words, thus creating new powers and new rights totally at odds with the logic of our Constitution and its commitment to the rule of law." Constitutional originalism entailed a rule of law that had a fixed meaning and therefore a fixed expectation on the part of citizens regarding their rights.[18]

A few months later, Justice William J. Brennan Jr. took direct aim at "those who find legitimacy in fidelity to what they call 'the intentions of the Framers.'" In a speech delivered at Georgetown University's Text and Teaching Symposium, he argued that "the genius of the Constitution rests not in any static meaning it might have had in a world that is dead and gone, but in the adaptability of its great principles to cope with current problems and current needs." He thought it was "arrogant" for anyone to claim to know precisely what "the intent of the Framers" was, let alone apply it to current matters of state. "What the constitutional fundamentals meant to the wisdom of other times," Brennan added, "cannot be their measure to the vision of our time." Nevertheless, despite the "evolutionary process" of interpreting the Constitution, he discerned a "constitutional ideal of human dignity" that did not change over time and therefore should inform each generation's "constitutional vision." In this way, Brennan actually agreed with Meese in discerning an "essential meaning" in the Constitution, despite its being written so long ago, and in believing it contained "fundamental values" that should inspire each generation of Americans.[19]

Acknowledging that justices are not perfect, Brennan nevertheless believed the court should act as if they were perfect because they stood as the last resort on constitutional questions: "We Justices are certainly aware that we are not final because we are infallible; we know that we are infallible only because we are final." This debate over what role the past should play in contemporary interpretations of the Constitution continues to this day as the Supreme Court divides between justices who seek "the original meaning of constitutional provisions" and justices who argue for a Constitution that must "evolve"—what is now called a "living Constitution"—and therefore in need of the court's guidance about what direction that evolution should take.[20]

Debating whether to follow the founders' intentions has never been an abstract quarrel over some constitutional nicety. Lincoln believed the future of freedom and slavery in the United States would be determined by either his or Stephen Douglas's policy regarding congressional authority over the expansion of slavery. As shown earlier, Lincoln believed the achievements of the fathers could scarcely be improved on, but he was not alone in tying his principles and policies to the founding generation. Stephen Douglas also claimed that he was the true interpreter and supporter of the founders' legacy. Employing the language of the "fathers," he claimed throughout his 1858 debates with Lincoln that his policy of local popular sovereignty best reflected the founders' intentions: "Our fathers intended that our institutions should differ. They knew that the North and the South having different climates, productions and interests, required different institutions." Douglas thought the founders wanted to preserve the American states in all their diversity and hence had no expectation of slavery's demise. He had no problem with a federal government that would remain indifferent to the enslavement of people he considered "inferior and dependent being[s]."[21]

Douglas argued that Lincoln would replace the founders' intention to preserve the "diversity in the local institutions and law," which allowed for "free and slave states," with a crude "uniformity in the local laws and domestic institutions," meaning that the states must become all free or all slave. Douglas claimed it was "a new doctrine, never dreamed of by Washington, Madison, or the framers of this Government," and one that presumed Lincoln and the Republicans were "wiser than these men who made this government." Douglas believed the federal government had "flourished for seventy years under the principle of popular sovereignty, recognizing the right of each State to do as it pleased." Douglas observed, "When this government was established by Washington, Jefferson, Madison, Jay, Hamilton, Franklin, and the other sages and patriots of that day, it was composed of free States and slave States, bound together by one common constitution." He saw no reason why it could not "endure divided into free and slave States, as our fathers made it." This contradicted Lincoln's claim that agitation over slavery would cease only if the nation became all free or all slave. Douglas argued that pressing for such uniformity would, instead, lead to war. He thought that only by remaining diverse, comprising both free and slave states indefinitely into the future, could America preserve peace and unity and be able to expand and prosper.[22]

Lincoln countered Douglas's claim to the mantle of the founders, especially regarding what to do about slavery. He did not think that putting slavery "upon the original basis—the basis upon which our fathers placed it" would have "any tendency to set the Northern and the Southern States at war with one another." Lincoln disagreed with Douglas, as well as Chief Justice Taney, about the "the original basis" or approach of the founders toward slavery. He argued that Douglas's Kansas-Nebraska Act contradicted "these 'original principles'" and believed he had been "fighting it in the Jeffersonian, Washingtonian, and Madisonian fashion." The outcome of his debate with Douglas would soon play out in the 1860 presidential election when their opposing policies confronted John Breckenridge and the Southern Democrats' defense of the right to own slaves in federal territory. Lincoln believed returning to the founders' approach to slavery would preserve a union "worthy of the saving" without war. On November 6, 1860, Americans south of the Mason-Dixon Line rejected Lincoln's interpretation of the founders and soon adopted a new constitution that made "the right of property in negro slaves" the cornerstone of their new confederacy and the fundamental reason they started a war to establish a separate nation.[23]

Perhaps Lincoln's most controversial claim about following the intentions of the founders occurred when he suspended the privilege of the writ of habeas corpus during the war. He gave an apt description of the suspension: "to arrest, and detain, without resort to the ordinary processes and forms of law, such individuals as he might deem dangerous to the public safety." Lincoln justified his decision to suspend the privilege by a constitutional logic he traced to the founders' original decision to establish a self-governing regime. In both the United States and England (where the privilege originated), the traditional understanding of the writ of habeas corpus saw it as a protection against arbitrary executive imprisonment of individuals.

The principal means of securing that protection against executive abuse was legislative action. In the case of the United States, the constitutional provision addressing when that privilege could be suspended is found in Article I, Section 9: it lays out restrictions of Congress's authority and never explicitly mentions the president, whose authority and limitations are spelled out mostly in Article II. However, Lincoln observed that the Constitution was "silent as to which, or who, is to exercise the power." It simply spelled out when the privilege could be suspended: "when, in cases of rebellion or invasion, the public safety may require it."[24]

Lincoln then argued that from the Constitution's end, the means must have been part of the design of the Constitution, which left ambiguous which branch of the federal government would have the authority to suspend the privilege in the event of an emergency. Here the Constitution was explicit about *when* this authority could be exercised and less clear about *who* would decide if an emergency existed. Lincoln concluded that "as the provision was plainly made for a dangerous emergency, it cannot be believed the framers of the instrument intended that in every case the danger should run its course until Congress could be called together; the very assembling of which might be prevented, as was intended in this case, by the rebellion." He appealed to the Constitution's framers not by citing a record of their debate in the summer of 1787 or contemporaneous letters or newspaper editorials like the *Federalist Papers*. Instead, he inferred their intention from a provision they designed to address an extraordinary situation, one that could not always be addressed by a national legislature given that it would not always be in session. On those rare occasions, only the executive would be able to meet the danger and thereby fulfill the Constitution's purposes.[25]

Lincoln's reasoning from an original intention of constitutional ends or purposes invited significant criticism. Historical precedent and constitutional commentary, in both America and England, saw the legislature as the sole, legitimate authority to suspend a right that was a long-standing protection against executive abuse of prerogative. Nevertheless, Lincoln and his attorney general, Edward Bates (whose opinion Lincoln requested), made the most of the constitutional silence regarding which branch possessed this authority. Although the constitutional provision is found in Article I, which primarily but not exclusively addresses the authority of Congress, it does not expressly state that Congress possessed this authority. Lincoln thought it was less important where the provision was found and more important that the intention of the Constitution—in anticipating that an occasion may arise that calls for the denial of the privilege—be followed for the good of the nation.[26]

Lincoln's focus on constitutional ends showed how to interpret and apply the specific means spelled out in the Constitution. As he noted in his July 4, 1861, Speech to Congress in Special Session, in which he rejected a constitutional right to secede, "nothing should ever be implied as law which leads to unjust or absurd consequences." He noted that the "legality and propriety" of his suspension of the privilege had been "questioned" and granted that "the one who is sworn to 'take care that the laws be faithfully executed' should not himself violate them." After reciting the actions he took while Congress was out of session in the early months of the war, he then asked, "Must a Government, of necessity, be too *strong* for the liberties of its own people, or too *weak* to maintain its own existence?" Here Lincoln presented the spectrum of executive authority when faced with an unprecedented threat to the nation's existence, as well as to the very idea of constitutional self-government. By doing so, he hoped to equip the American people to judge whether his response to armed secession prudently avoided extremes that would destroy free government not only in America but also the world.[27]

By highlighting the connection between constitutional means and ends, Lincoln taught the American people that how they govern themselves is as important as the ends to which they govern. In the case of the American founding, the citizens' original intention to live as a free people reposed in them an abiding responsibility to understand the nature of their free institutions and the practices necessary for the successful perpetuation of those institutions. By consistently harking back to their original intentions, both in principle and in practice, Lincoln invited Americans to consider the merits of that founding in light of challenges that offered alternative interpretations—not all of which were sympathetic to the found-ers' original intentions. In Lincoln, one finds no blind follower of the American founding but a thoughtful and thought-provoking citizen who became a statesman by inviting all Americans to be-lieve that what the founders had achieved was the best, most pru-dent, and therefore most relevant means of securing their safety and happiness.[28]

CONCLUSION: LINCOLN AS CONSERVATIVE LIBERAL OR LIBERAL CONSERVATIVE?

What is conservatism? Preserving the old against the new.
—Abraham Lincoln, Speech at Leavenworth, Kansas (1859)

Early in the 1860 election year, Lincoln defended Republicans from Southern claims that they were "revolutionary" in their aims. The main criticism was the party's insistence that Congress prohibit slavery in the federal territories despite the Supreme Court's ruling in *Dred Scott v. Sanford* that Congress had no authority to do so. Lincoln argued, "But you say you are conservative—eminently conservative—while we are revolutionary, destructive, or something of the sort. What is conservatism? Is it not adherence to the old and tried, against the new and untried?"[1] Lincoln rebutted the charge that the Republican Party was radical because it tried to stop the spread of slavery. As a champion of the liberal principles of the founding and the constitutional means to securing those principles, Lincoln sought to conserve those old ways of understanding human nature, civil society, and the purpose of government. In doing so, he fought off rhetorically, and then with military force, attempts to implement alternative means to alternative ends of protecting rights in the United States. As Lincoln's law partner William Herndon observed, "Had it not been for his conservative statesmanship, . . . this nation might have been two governments to-day."[2]

Inherent in Lincoln's conservatism was his conviction that the American founding was liberal at its core. By the end of the Civil War, he believed progress in securing liberty would come only if the nation fulfilled the original promise of its founding, "that all men are created equal." In the words of the British biographer Lord Charnwood, Lincoln's public life sought "the restoration of his country to its earliest and noblest tradition, which alone gave permanence or worth to its existence as a nation." By the time of his generation, Lincoln saw America's oldest tradition as its noblest, and Charnwood highlighted this happy coincidence of the American founding to show that Lincoln loved his country not merely because it was his but also because it was good.[3]

In this Lincoln imitated fellow Whig Henry Clay, of whom Lincoln remarked in an 1852 eulogy, "He loved his country partly because it was his own country, but mostly because it was a free country." Lincoln highlighted his "deep devotion to the cause of human liberty" as the engine of Clay's efforts to preserve the American union: "Feeling, as he did, and as the truth surely is, that the world's best hope depended on the continued Union of these States, he was ever jealous of, and watchful for, whatever might have the slightest tendency to separate them." Two years later, with the passage of the Kansas-Nebraska Act, the nation was tempted to forget that the American states formed a union for the sake of human liberty. This inspired Lincoln to jump back into politics with both feet, where he found his surest footing promoting policies based on the principles and practices of the founding. For the next six years, Lincoln presented the country with a clear choice regarding the future of slavery. He not only dashed Stephen Douglas's hopes for the presidency but also helped the nation reclaim its founding principles as "the last best, hope of earth."[4]

Lincoln consistently expressed this philanthropic view of the success of American self-government. He believed that the principles of the American founding were universal and therefore the basis on which any people the world over could become free. His determination to preserve the American union in the face of sectional rebellion was not simply a war of self-defense but also an effort to vindicate the capacity of a free people to rule themselves. In 1852, Lincoln joined fellow Whigs in calling for the recognition of Hungarians fighting for a free Hungary as a way to affirm "our continued devotion to the principles of our free institutions." In 1862, hosting the minister from San Salvador (present-day Costa Rica), Lincoln described Union victory as a boon for loyal Americans and "the progress, civilization, and happiness of mankind." He was hopeful that a free America could demonstrate its ability to put down a rebellion and therefore prove "its adaptation to the highest interests of society—the preservation of the State itself against the violence of faction." He added, "Elsewhere on the American continent it is struggling against the inroads of anarchy, which invites foreign intervention." Whether commenting on the internal strife of the United States or the struggles throughout Central and South America to secure freedom, independence, and stability in the region, Lincoln encouraged the efforts for freedom at home and abroad. "Let the American States," he declared, "therefore, draw closer together and animate and reassure each other, and thus prove to the world that, although we have inherited some of the errors of ancient systems, we are nevertheless capable of completing and establishing the new one which we have now chosen." The great presumption of the Old World was that a free people were incapable of ruling themselves, which justified dividing society into despots and subjects, masters and slaves. Lincoln believed that in defending self-government in the Western Hemisphere, the United States and its like-minded neighbors could dissuade enemies both foreign and domestic from disrupting the march of freedom in the world.[5]

After issuing the Emancipation Proclamation, Lincoln defended the Union war effort as a way "to save and strengthen the foundations of our national unity." The preservation of the United States, which required the abolition of slavery, would produce a stronger nation by eliminating a way of thinking about freedom that was subversive of the American regime. Before the war, Lincoln tried to persuade white Americans to reject a slaveholding mentality as the first step to eliminating the enslavement of black people in the long run. He encouraged them to "HAVE FAITH THAT RIGHT MAKES MIGHT." This appeal was not simply an exhortation to citizens in 1860 to vote the

Republican ticket, as many had done in 1856, without concern that they would be wasting their vote. It also expressed a conviction that to do otherwise would be to reject their ancient faith, the faith of their fathers in the human capacity for self-government. The alternative would transform America's original commitment to individual rights into a mere expression of majority might, whether through Stephen Douglas's popular sovereignty or John Calhoun's "positive good" school of black slavery. For both Douglas and Calhoun, mere self-interest became the *summum bonum* of American self-government. Lincoln's task was to persuade Americans that protecting the rights of all members of their community would provide the greatest security for their own rights. For him, despite their tolerance of black slavery, the founders pointed the way.[6]

As Lincoln understood them, the founders declared independence on the basis of a standard that would be the measure of their own faithfulness to the principles of self-government. President William Clinton stated this well in his First Inaugural Address: "Our democracy must be not only the envy of the world but the engine of our own renewal. There is nothing wrong with America that cannot be cured by what is right with America."[7] This identification of American progress with old American standards, not new ones, has marked the nation's greatest movements for social and political progress, as well. For example, it was the modern civil rights movement's *cri de coeur*, as shown in Martin Luther King Jr.'s last speech: "All we say to America is, 'Be true to what you said on paper.'" King had previously identified that "paper" as the Declaration of Independence and the U.S. Constitution and described them as "a promissory note to which every American was to fall heir." Without this appeal to the American founding as a way to measure the gap between profession and practice, one wonders how else progress would have been marked in American history.[8]

It was once said of Lincoln during the last year of his presidency, "There stands a man who combines in his person all that is valuable in *progress* in conservatism—all that is hopeful in *progress*."[9] For Lincoln, progress in conservatism would entail a renewed respect for the founders and a return to their approach to policy, which was based on the natural rights of human beings. To be "hopeful in progress" would mean an expectation that the future would be better than the past, but precisely because that future was made possible by an old but true understanding of human nature and civil society. Lincoln leaned on the founding for help in his times, convinced that conserving the founders' ways offered later generations the best chance to enjoy liberty. He was conservative for the sake of liberty, which may explain his subsequent appeal across the political spectrum. By looking to America's past, Lincoln taught the nation the importance of civic memory in perpetuating self-government. Whether conservative or liberal, Lincoln's appeal to the American founders restores their relevance to future generations and helps ensure "that government of the people, by the people, for the people shall not perish from the earth."

ACKNOWLEDGMENTS
NOTES
BIBLIOGRAPHY
INDEX

ACKNOWLEDGMENTS

My first words of thanks go to Sylvia Frank Rodrigue and Richard W. Etulain. Without their invitation to propose a topic for the Concise Lincoln Library Series and patience with me as I finally got the manuscript completed, it would not have come to fruition. I especially appreciate Dick's editorial suggestions and Joyce Bond's careful perusal. Their guidance helped me revise the manuscript in a way that I hope readers will find both readable and scholarly.

I am grateful for the support of Washington and Lee University, in particular, Robert D. Straughan, dean of the Williams School of Commerce, Economics, and Politics, and Provost Marc C. Conner, administrator of the Lenfest Summer Grants program, which supported the research and writing of the book. I also thank the Ashbrook Center at Ashland University for supporting my work ever since I was a graduate student. With its commitment to the enrichment of high school and middle school teaching of American history, the center is a model for teaching constitutional self-government, promoting civic education, and inspiring love of the American way of life.

Last, I thank my wife, Cherie, and children, Luke, Hannah, Ellison, and Natalie, for their abiding love and support as I studied America's greatest defender, Abraham Lincoln. I trust they will think this book was worth all the effort.

NOTES

Introduction: Looking to the Past for the Sake of the Future

1. For a discussion of the centrality of the founding for subsequent generations of Americans, see James W. Ceaser, "The First American Founder," *National Affairs* 36 (Summer 2018), https://www.nationalaffairs.com /publications/detail/the-first-american-founder (accessed November 5, 2019).

2. Robert Bray, *Reading with Lincoln* (Carbondale: Southern Illinois University Press, 2010), 4, 10, 13, 23–27, 226; Abraham Lincoln, "Speech at Cincinnati, Ohio," September 17, 1859, in *The Collected Works of Abraham Lincoln*, ed. Roy P. Basler (New Brunswick, NJ: Rutgers University, 1953), 3:453; Lincoln, "Speech at Carlinville, Illinois," August 31, 1858, *Collected Works*, 3:78.

3. Woodrow Wilson, "The Author and Signers of the Declaration," September 1907, *Woodrow Wilson: The Essential Political Writings*, ed. Ronald J. Pestritto (Lanham, MD: Lexington Books, 2005), 99–100, 97, 99.

4. Lincoln, "To Henry L. Pierce and Others," April 6, 1859, *Collected Works*, 3:376.

1. Lincoln, George Washington, and the Founding Fathers: An Appeal to the Founder Par Excellence

1. Henry Knox, "From Brigadier General Henry Knox," November 26, 1777, in *The Papers of George Washington*, Revolutionary War Series, vol. 12, *October 1777–December 1777*, ed. Frank E. Grizzard Jr. and David R. Hoth (Charlottesville: University of Virginia Press, 2002), 415.

2. Lord Byron, "Personal, Lyric, and Elegiac Ode to Napoleon Buonaparte," In *Poetry of Byron, Chosen and Arranged by Matthew Arnold* (London: Macmillan, 1881); Bartleby.com, 2013, https://www.bartleby .com/205/31.html (accessed April 23, 2019).

3. Daniel Webster, *The Bunker Hill Monument, Adams and Jefferson: Two Orations* (Boston: Houghton, Mifflin, 1893), 13, 35, https://archive.org /stream/bunkerhillmonum01websgoog#page/n6/mode/2up (accessed April 23, 2019); Lincoln, "Address before the Young Men's Lyceum of Springfield, Illinois," January 27, 1838, *Collected Works*, 1:115 (emphasis in original unless otherwise noted). All quoted material from Lincoln appears as it did in the original, including misspellings and any apparent errors of grammar, syntax, and punctuation. Cf. President Martin Van Buren's First Inaugural Address of March 4, 1837, which did not foresee any major threat to popular government, at https://www.gutenberg

.org/files/925/925-h/925-h.htm#link2H_4_0013 (accessed November 4, 2019).

4. Lincoln, "Address before the Young Men's Lyceum of Springfield, Illinois," January 27, 1838, *Collected Works*, 1:108.

5. Ibid., 1:113.

6. Ibid., 1:114, 113, 108; Webster, *Bunker Hill Monument*, 35, 36.

7. Lincoln, "Address before the Young Men's Lyceum of Springfield, Illinois," January 27, 1838, *Collected Works*, 1:114, 113, 108.

8. Ibid., 1:114, 112.

9. Webster, *Bunker Hill Monument*, 13, 14; Lincoln, "Address before the Young Men's Lyceum of Springfield, Illinois," January 27, 1838, *Collected Works*, 1:109, 115, 114.

10. Webster, *Bunker Hill Monument*, 35, 14; Lincoln, "Annual Message to Congress," December 1, 1862, *Collected Works*, 5:537; Lincoln, "Address before the Young Men's Lyceum of Springfield, Illinois," January 27, 1838, *Collected Works*, 1:115.

11. Lincoln, "Address before the Young Men's Lyceum of Springfield, Illinois," January 27, 1838, *Collected Works*, 1:115; Lincoln, "Second Speech at Frederick, Maryland," October 4, 1862, *Collected Works*, 5:450.

12. Lincoln, "Address to the New Jersey Senate at Trenton, New Jersey," February 21, 1861, *Collected Works*, 4:235. For the text of the notorious biography of Washington, see Mason L. Weems, *The Life of Washington*, intro. Peter S. Onuf (New York: Routledge, 1996).

13. Lincoln, "Address to the New Jersey Senate at Trenton, New Jersey," February 21, 1861, *Collected Works*, 4:236.

14. Lincoln, "Speech in Independence Hall, Philadelphia, Pennsylvania," February 22, 1861, *Collected Works*, 4:240.

15. Lincoln, "Farewell Address at Springfield, Illinois," February 11, 1861, *Collected Works*, 4:190. For Lincoln's drafting and delivery of the speech and subsequent revision on the train out of town, see Douglas L. Wilson, *Lincoln's Sword: The Presidency and the Power of Words* (New York: Alfred A. Knopf, 2006), 10–18.

16. Lincoln, "Farewell Address at Springfield, Illinois," February 11, 1861, *Collected Works*, 4:190.

17. Lincoln, "First Inaugural Address," March 4, 1861, *Collected Works*, 4:270; Lincoln, "Message to Congress in Special Session," July 4, 1861, *Collected Works*, 4:441; and Lincoln, "Annual Message to Congress," December 3, 1861, *Collected Works*, 5:53. See also Lincoln, "Meditation on the Divine Will," [September 2, 1862?], *Collected Works*, 5:404. His most famous reflection on God's purposes in the Civil War is his Second Inaugural Address. For a discussion of his belief in a personal God, see

Samuel W. Calhoun and Lucas E. Morel, "Abraham Lincoln's Religion: The Case for His Ultimate Belief in a Personal, Sovereign God," *Journal of the Abraham Lincoln Association* 33, no. 1 (Winter 2012): 38–74.

18. Lincoln, "To Alexander Reed," February 22, 1863, *Collected Works*, 6:114–15; Lincoln, "Order for Sabbath Observance," November 15, 1862, *Collected Works*, 5:497–98. Representative Edward Haight of New York proposed the idea to Lincoln five days before Washington's birthday. Lincoln, "Order for Sabbath Observance," November 15, 1862, *Collected Works*, 5:498n1. See also Lincoln, "Proclamation for Celebration of Washington's Birthday," February 19, 1862, *Collected Works*, 5:136–37.

19. Lincoln, "Temperance Address," February 22, 1842, *Collected Works*, 1:279; Lincoln, "To Taylor Committee" (February 9, 1848), *Collected Works*, 1:449–50n2. See Martin H. Quitt, "In the Shadow of the Little Giant: Lincoln before the Great Debates," *Journal of the Abraham Lincoln Association* 36, no. 1 (Winter 2015): 28.

20. Lincoln, "Speech in United States House of Representatives: The War with Mexico," January 12, 1848, *Collected Works*, 1:439. For Lincoln's specific charges regarding President Polk's claims about the location of the initial hostilities with Mexico, see Lincoln, "'Spot' Resolutions in the United States House of Representatives," December 22, 1847, *Collected Works*, 1:420–22.

21. George Washington, "Circular to the States," June 14, 1783, in *George Washington: A Collection*, ed. W. B. Allen (Indianapolis: Liberty Fund, 1988), 244.

22. Lincoln, "To John M. Peck," May 21, 1848, *Collected Works*, 1:473.

23. Lincoln, "Proclamation Calling Militia and Convening Congress," April 15, 1861, *Collected Works*, 4:332; cf. George Washington, "Proclamation," August 7, 1786, in *George Washington*, 589–92.

24. For the circumstances surrounding Baltimore's reaction to federal troops, see Jonathan W. White, *Abraham Lincoln and Treason in the Civil War: The Trials of John Merryman* (Baton Rouge: Louisiana State University Press, 2011), 10–24.

25. Form letter of Secretary of War Simon Cameron to state governors dated April 15, 1861. Maryland's total, including a brigadier general and 151 officers, amounted to 3,123 men. For letter and table, see Simon Cameron, Form Letter of the Secretary of War to State Governors, April 15, 1861, *The Civil War and Northwest Wisconsin* (blog), https://the civilwarandnorthwestwisconsin.wordpress.com/2011/04/15/1861-april -15-lincolns-call-for-troops/ (accessed April 23, 2019).

26. Lincoln, "Reply to Baltimore Committee," April 22, 1861, *Collected Works*, 4:341–42.

27. Lincoln, "Speech at Vandalia, Illinois," September 23, 1856, *Collected Works*, 2:378.

28. For a description of the founding of the Republican Party that links its purpose to the purpose of the American founding, see Forrest A. Nabors, *From Oligarchy to Republicanism: The Great Task of Reconstruction* (Columbia: University of Missouri Press, 2017), 199–208.

29. Lincoln, "Address at Cooper Institute, New York City," February 22, 1860, *Collected Works*, 3:536–37.

30. Ibid.

31. Ibid., 3:550.

32. Stephen A. Douglas, "First Debate with Stephen A. Douglas at Ottawa, Illinois," August 21, 1858, *Collected Works*, 3:12, 8; Stephen A. Douglas, "Invasion of States," Cong. Globe, Senate, 36th Cong., 1st Sess. 554 (1860). For an insightful examination of the political contest over the proper heirs of the founders during the 1850s and 1860s, see Jeffrey J. Malanson, "The Founding Fathers and the Election of 1864," *Journal of Abraham Lincoln Association* 36, no. 2 (Summer 2015): 1–25.

33. See Harold Holzer, *Lincoln at Cooper Union: The Speech That Made Abraham Lincoln President* (New York: Simon & Schuster, 2004).

34. Lincoln, "Message to Congress in Special Session," July 4, 1861, *Collected Works*, 4:438–39.

35. Ibid., 4:438.

36. Lincoln, "Speech on the Sub-Treasury," December [26], 1839, *Collected Works*, 1:170.

37. Lincoln, "Speech at Chicago, Illinois," July 10, 1858, *Collected Works*, 2:499.

38. Zachary Taylor did not appeal to the nation's "fathers" or "forefathers" but did call George Washington "the Father of his country." Zachary Taylor, "Inaugural Address," March 5, 1849, http://avalon.law.yale.edu/19th_century/taylor.asp (accessed April 23, 2019).

39. Stephen A. Douglas, "First Debate with Stephen A. Douglas at Ottawa, Illinois," August 21, 1858, *Collected Works*, 3:8; Stephen A. Douglas, "Fifth Debate with Stephen A. Douglas at Galesburg, Illinois," October 7, 1858, *Collected Works*, 3:216. See also Stephen A. Douglas, "Third Debate with Stephen A. Douglas at Jonesboro, Illinois," September 15, 1858, *Collected Works*, 3: 112–13; "Fourth Debate with Stephen A. Douglas at Charleston, Illinois," September 18, 1858, *Collected Works*, 3:177–78; "Seventh and Last Debate with Stephen A. Douglas at Alton, Illinois," October 15, 1858, *Collected Works*, 3:296, 322.

40. Stephen A. Douglas, "Douglas at Chicago, July 9, 1858," in Paul M. Angle, ed., *Created Equal? The Complete Lincoln-Douglas Debates of 1858* (1958; repr., Chicago: Midway, 1985), 18–20.

41. Ibid., 21; Dred Scott v. Sanford (1857), 60 U.S. 393, 450–52.

42. Lincoln, "Speech at Chicago, Illinois," July 10, 1858, *Collected Works*, 2:492; Lincoln, "Speech at Springfield, Illinois," July 17, 1858, *Collected Works*, 2:515.

43. Lincoln, "Third Debate with Stephen A. Douglas at Jonesboro, Illinois," September 15, 1858, *Collected Works*, 3:117; Douglas, "Douglas at Chicago, July 9, 1858," in Angle, *Created Equal?* 18; Lincoln, "Seventh and Last Debate with Stephen A. Douglas at Alton, Illinois," October 15, 1858, *Collected Works*, 3:313, 315.

44. Lincoln, "Speech at Columbus, Ohio," September 16, 1859, *Collected Works*, 3:407; Lincoln, "Address at Cooper Institute, New York City," February 22, 1860, *Collected Works*, 3:535.

45. Lincoln, "Address Delivered at the Dedication of the Cemetery at Gettysburg," November 19, 1863, *Collected Works*, 7:23.

46. Lincoln, "Emancipation Proclamation," January 1, 1863, *Collected Works*, 6:29; Lincoln, "Address Delivered at the Dedication of the Cemetery at Gettysburg," November 19, 1863, *Collected Works*, 7:23.

47. Richard Brookhiser, *Founders' Son: A Life of Abraham Lincoln* (New York: Basic Books, 2014), 244. See also Bradley C. S. Watson, *Living Constitution, Dying Faith: Progressivism and the New Science of Jurisprudence* (Wilmington, DE: ISI Books, 2009), 47, and 38–53, generally.

48. Lincoln, "To Joseph H. Choate," December 19, 1864, *Collected Works*, 8:170.

2. Lincoln and the Declaration of Independence: An Appeal to the Founders' Ends

1. Lincoln, "Speech at Chicago, Illinois," July 10, 1858, *Collected Works*, 2:499, 492.

2. All quotes from the Bible are from the King James Version (KJV) unless otherwise noted.

3. Lincoln, "Speech at Chicago, Illinois," July 10, 1858, *Collected Works*, 2:499–500.

4. See Gary Ecelbarger, *The Great Comeback: How Abraham Lincoln Beat the Odds to Win the 1860 Republican Nomination* (New York: St. Martin's Press, 2008), 34. Also see Lincoln, "Call for Republican Meeting," April 11, 1859, *Collected Works*, 3:377, which announced a mass meeting of Republicans for April 13, which was the same day as the Boston festival honoring Jefferson.

5. Lincoln, "To Henry L. Pierce and Others," April 6, 1859, *Collected Works*, 3:375; Lincoln, "Autobiography Written for John L. Scripps," [ca. June, 1860], *Collected Works*, 4:62.

6. Lincoln, "To Henry L. Pierce and Others," April 6, 1859, *Collected Works*, 3:376; Lincoln, "Speech at Columbus, Ohio," September 16, 1859, *Collected Works*, 3:410.

7. William Herndon to Ward Hill Lamon (March 3, 1870), in William H. Herndon, *Herndon on Lincoln: Letters*, ed. Douglas L. Wilson and Rodney O. Davis (Urbana: Knox College Lincoln Studies Center and the University of Illinois Press, 2016), 94; Lincoln, "To James H. Reed," October 1, 1860, *Collected Works*, 4:124.

8. Lincoln, "To Anson G. Chester," September 5, 1860, *Collected Works*, 4:111; Lincoln, "Speech at Peoria, Illinois," October 16, 1854, *Collected Works*, 2:249; *United States Congress, March 1, 1784, Printed Resolution on Western Territory Government; with Notations by Thomas Jefferson*, Thomas Jefferson Papers at the Library of Congress, Manuscript Division, http://hdl.loc.gov/loc.mss/mtj.mtjbib000873 (accessed November 5, 2019); Lincoln, "Speech at Carlinville, Illinois," August 31, 1858, *Collected Works*, 3:79–80.

9. See Thomas Jefferson, "To John Holmes," April 22, 1820, in *The Portable Thomas Jefferson*, ed. Merrill D. Peterson (New York: Penguin Books, 1975), 568 (Jefferson's emphasis). For a lucid interpretation of Jefferson's diffusion thesis in light of his earlier proposal of nonextension of slavery, see Thomas W. Merrill, "The Later Jefferson and the Problem of Natural Rights," in *The Political Thought of the Civil War*, ed. Alan Levine, Thomas W. Merrill, and James R. Stoner Jr. (Lawrence: University Press of Kansas, 2018), 27–44.

10. Lincoln, "Speech at Peoria, Illinois," October 16, 1854, *Collected Works*, 2:263–64.

11. See Danielle Allen, *Our Declaration: A Reading of the Declaration of Independence in Defense of Equality* (New York: W. W. Norton, 2014), 112; Pauline Maier, *American Scripture: Making the Declaration of Independence* (New York: Alfred A. Knopf, 1997), 87; Bernard Bailyn, *The Ideological Origins of the American Revolution* (Cambridge, MA: Harvard University Press, 1967), 27.

12. Thomas Jefferson, "To John Trumbull," February 15, 1789, *Portable Thomas Jefferson*, 435; Thomas Jefferson, "To Richard Henry Lee," May 8, 1825, quoted in Jeremy D. Bailey, *Thomas Jefferson and Executive Power* (New York: Cambridge University Press, 2007), 106.

13. Bray, *Reading with Lincoln*, 226, cites Jefferson's *Works*, volumes 4, 7–9, as the source of Lincoln's specific reading of Jefferson's writings; see Thomas Jefferson, *The Writings of Thomas Jefferson*, ed. H. A. Washington, 9 vols. (New York: J. C. Riker, 1853–55).

14. Lincoln, "Speech in Independence Hall, Philadelphia, Pennsylvania," February 22, 1861, *Collected Works*, 4:240; Lee Resolution showing

congressional vote, July 2, 1776; Papers of the Continental Congress, 1774–1783; Records of the Continental and Confederation Congresses and the Constitutional Convention, 1774–1789, Record Group 360; National Archive, https://www.ourdocuments.gov/doc.php?flash=false &doc=1 (accessed November 5, 2019).

15. Lincoln, "Speech in Independence Hall, Philadelphia, Pennsylvania," February 22, 1861, *Collected Works*, 4:240.

16. Ibid.; Lincoln, "Speech at Springfield, Illinois," June 26, 1857, *Collected Works*, 2:407.

17. Lincoln, "Speech in Independence Hall, Philadelphia, Pennsylvania," February 22, 1861, *Collected Works*, 4:240, 241.

18. John Locke, *Second Treatise of Government* [1690], ed. C. B. Macpherson (Indianapolis: Hackett, 1980), chap. 2, sec. 4, p. 8.

19. Lincoln, "Speech at Peoria, Illinois," October 16, 1854, *Collected Works*, 2:265; Lincoln quoting Henry Clay, "Seventh and Last Debate with Stephen A. Douglas at Alton, Illinois," October 15, 1858, *Collected Works*, 3:304 (Clay's emphasis); and Lincoln, "Letter to James N. Brown," October 18, 1858, *Collected Works*, 3:328.

20. Lincoln, "Speech at Peoria, Illinois," October 16, 1854, *Collected Works*, 2:265.

21. Lincoln, "Speech at Carlinville, Illinois," August 31, 1858, *Collected Works*, 3:78.

22. Lincoln, "Speech at Peoria, Illinois," October 16, 1854, *Collected Works*, 2:265.

23. Stephen A. Douglas, "Nebraska Territory," Cong. Globe, Senate, 33rd Cong., 1st Sess. 275 (1854).

24. Lincoln, "Speech at Peoria, Illinois," October 16, 1854, *Collected Works*, 2:266.

25. Ibid., 2:250, 266, 275, 276.

26. Ibid., 2:276.

27. Ibid. See also Lincoln, "Speech at a Republican Banquet, Chicago, Illinois," December 10, 1856, *Collected Works*, 2:385.

28. Lincoln, "Speech at Peoria, Illinois," October 16, 1854, *Collected Works*, 2:276.

29. Lincoln, "Speech at Lewistown, Illinois," August 17, 1858, *Collected Works*, 2:546; Lincoln, "Stay of Execution for Nathaniel Gordon," February 4, 1862, *Collected Works*, 5:128. For a riveting account of this unique episode in American history, see Ron Soodalter, *Hanging Nathaniel Gordon: The Life and Trial of an American Slave Trader* (New York: Atria, 2006).

30. Lincoln, "Address Delivered at the Dedication of the Cemetery at Gettysburg," November 19, 1863, *Collected Works*, 7:23.

31. Ibid.

32. Lincoln, "Speech at a Republican Banquet, Chicago, Illinois," December 10, 1856, Collected Works, 2:385.

33. Lincoln, "Speech at Springfield, Illinois," June 26, 1857, *Collected Works*, 2:405.

34. Ibid. For the development of voting rights in America, see Alexander Keyssar, *The Right to Vote: The Contested History of Democracy in the United States*, rev. ed. (2000; repr., New York: Basic Books, 2009).

35. Lincoln, "Speech at Springfield, Illinois," June 26, 1857, *Collected Works*, 2:405–6.

36. Lincoln, "First Debate with Stephen A. Douglas at Ottawa, Illinois," August 21, 1858, *Collected Works*, 3:16. For an examination of Lincoln's arguments regarding race in contrast with those of Stephen Douglas, see Lucas E. Morel, "Lincoln, Race, and the Spirit of '76," *Perspectives in Political Science* 39, no. 1 (2010): 3–11. For an incisive interpretation of Lincoln's speech against the *Dred Scott* decision, see Diana Schaub, "Lincoln and the Daughters of Dred Scott: A Reflection on the Declaration of Independence," in *When in the Course of Human Events: 1776 at Home, Abroad, and in American Memory*, ed. Will R. Jordon (Macon, GA: Mercer University Press, 2018), 189–210.

37. Thomas Jefferson, "To Henri Grégoire," February 25, 1809, *Portable Thomas Jefferson*, 517.

38. Lincoln, "Speech at Springfield, Illinois," June 26, 1857, *Collected Works*, 2:406.

39. Ibid.

40. Ibid., 2:405–7; Lincoln, "Speech at Chicago, Illinois," July 10, 1858, *Collected Works*, 2:500, 493.

41. Lincoln, "Address at Sanitary Fair, Baltimore, Maryland," April 18, 1864, *Collected Works*, 7:301–2.

42. See Harry V. Jaffa, "The Meaning of Equality: Abstract and Practical," chap. 17 in *Crisis of the House Divided: An Interpretation of the Issues in the Lincoln-Douglas Debates* (1959; repr., Chicago: University of Chicago Press, 1982), 363–86.

43. Lincoln, "Speech at Peoria, Illinois," October 16, 1854, *Collected Works*, 2:255, 266.

44. Thomas Jefferson, "First Inaugural Address," March 4, 1801, *Portable Thomas Jefferson*, 293; Lincoln, "Speech at Peoria, Illinois," October 16, 1854, *Collected Works*, 2:266.

45. Lincoln, "'A House Divided': Speech at Springfield, Illinois," June 16, 1858, *Collected Works*, 2:462.

46. Stephen A. Douglas, "Douglas at Springfield, July 17, 1858," in Angle, *Created Equal?* 54; Stephen A. Douglas, "Seventh and Last Debate

with Stephen A. Douglas at Alton, Illinois," October 15, 1858, *Collected Works*, 3:322.

47. Stephen A. Douglas, "First Debate with Stephen A. Douglas at Ottawa, Illinois," August 21, 1858, *Collected Works*, 3:10.

48. Lincoln, "Speech at Edwardsville, Illinois," September 11, 1858, *Collected Works*, 3:95.

49. Thomas Jefferson, "First Inaugural Address," March 4, 1801, *Portable Thomas Jefferson*, 291.

50. Lincoln, "To John A. Gilmer," December 15, 1860, *Collected Works*, 4:151, 152.

51. Lincoln, "Address to the New Jersey Senate at Trenton, New Jersey," February 21, 1861, *Collected Works*, 4:236. For details regarding Lincoln's visit to Trenton, see "Lincoln and New Jersey: A Bicentennial Tribute by the New Jersey State Archives," State of New Jersey Department of State, 2011, http://www.nj.gov/state/archives/lincoln.html (accessed November 5, 2019).

52. Lincoln, "To James T. Hale," January 11, 1861, *Collected Works*, 4:172. See also Lincoln, "Remarks Concerning Concessions to Secession," [ca. January 19–21, 1861], *Collected Works*, 4:175–76.

53. Lincoln, "Message to Congress in Special Session," July 4, 1861, *Collected Works*, 4:440.

54. Lincoln, "First Inaugural Address—First Edition and Revisions," March 4, 1861, *Collected Works*, 4:259. The fragility of American self-government in 1860 was forecast in 1856, as shown by John Bicknell, *Lincoln's Pathfinder: John C. Fremont and the Violent Election of 1856* (Chicago: Chicago Review Press, 2017).

55. See Locke, *Second Treatise*, secs. 224, 226, pp. 113–14.

56. Lincoln, "'Spot' Resolutions in the United States House of Representatives," December 22, 1847, *Collected Works*, 1:420–22; Lincoln, "Speech in United States House of Representatives: The War with Mexico" January 12, 1848, *Collected Works*, 1:438–39.

57. "South Carolina Declaration of the Causes of Secession," December 24, 1860, in *The Civil War: The First Year Told by Those Who Lived It*, ed. Brooks D. Simpson, Stephen W. Sears, and Aaron Sheehan-Dean (Washington, DC: Library of America, 2011), 153.

58. Lincoln, "First Inaugural Address," March 4, 1861, *Collected Works*, 4:265.

59. Ibid., 4:268, 265.

60. Thomas Jefferson, "First Inaugural Address," March 4, 1801, *Portable Thomas Jefferson*, 291.

61. Lincoln, "First Inaugural Address," March 4, 1861, *Collected Works*, 4:268; Lincoln, "Letter to Thurlow Weed," December 17, 1860, *Collected*

Works, 4:154; Lincoln, "Message to Congress in Special Session," July 4, 1861, *Collected Works*, 4:436.

62. Lincoln, "Proclamation Calling Militia and Convening Congress," April 15, 1861, *Collected Works*, 4:332; Lincoln, "Message to Congress in Special Session," July 4, 1861, *Collected Works*, 4:439.

63. Lincoln, "Message to Congress in Special Session," July 4, 1861, *Collected Works*, 4:432–33.

64. Lincoln, "Reply to the New York Workingmen's Democratic Republican Association," March 11, 1864, *Collected Works*, 7:259–60.

65. Lincoln, "Speech at Kalamazoo, Michigan," August 27, 1856, *Collected Works*, 2:364. For examples of Lincoln's exhortations of resolution and perseverance, see Lincoln, "To Isham Reavis," November 5, 1855, *Collected Works*, 2:327; Lincoln, "To Quintin Campbell," June 28, 1862, *Collected Works*, 5:289.

66. Lincoln, "Seventh and Last Debate with Stephen A. Douglas at Alton, Illinois," October 15, 1858, *Collected Works*, 3:304; Lincoln, "To Theodore Canisius," May 17, 1859, *Collected Works*, 3:380; Lincoln, "Letter to William H. Herndon," July 10, 1848, *Collected Works*, 1:497; Lincoln, "Fragment on Free Labor," [September 17, 1859?], *Collected Works*, 3:462–63.

67. Lincoln, "Fragment on Slavery," [April 1, 1854?], *Collected Works*, 2:222.

68. Lincoln, "Fragment on Pro-Slavery Theology," [October 1, 1858?], *Collected Works*, 3:204.

69. Lincoln, "Speech at New Haven, Connecticut," March 6, 1860, *Collected Works*, 4:24; Lincoln, "Address before the Wisconsin State Agricultural Society, Milwaukee, Wisconsin," September 30, 1859, *Collected Works*, 3:479–80.

70. Lincoln, "To John D. Johnston," November 4, 1851, *Collected Works*, 2:111; Lincoln, "To Thomas Lincoln and John D. Johnston," December 24, 1848, *Collected Works*, 2:16. Johnston died in 1854.

71. Lincoln, "To Jesse W. Fell, Enclosing Autobiography," December 20, 1859, *Collected Works*, 3:511. See also Daniel Walker Howe, "Why Abraham Lincoln Was a Whig," *Journal of the Abraham Lincoln Association* 16, no. 1 (Winter 1995): 30. For Lincoln's rough upbringing in Kentucky and Indiana, see Michael Burlingame, *Abraham Lincoln: A Life*, vol. 1 (Baltimore: Johns Hopkins University Press, 2008), chaps. 1–2.

72. Lincoln, "Speech to One-Hundred Sixty-Sixth Ohio Regiment," August 22, 1864, *Collected Works*, 7:512; Lincoln, "Speech to One-Hundred Forty-Eighth Ohio Regiment," August 31, 1864, *Collected Works*, 7:528. For the "right to rise," see Kenneth Winkle, *The Young Eagle: The Rise of Abraham Lincoln* (Dallas: Taylor Trade Publishing, 2001), 121–31.

73. Lincoln, "Message to Congress in Special Session," July 4, 1861, *Collected Works*, 4:439.

74. Lincoln, "Speech at Chicago, Illinois," July 10, 1858, *Collected Works*, 2:492.

75. Lincoln, "To Jesse W. Fell, Enclosing Autobiography," December 20, 1859, *Collected Works*, 3:512.

3. Lincoln and the Constitution: An Appeal to the Founders' Means

1. Alexander H. Stephens, "To Alexander H. Stephens," December 22, 1860, *Collected Works*, 4:161n1.

2. See, for example, Lincoln, "To Truman Smith," November 10, 1860, *Collected Works*, 4:138; Lincoln, "To Nathaniel P. Paschall," November 16, 1860, *Collected Works*, 4:139–40; Lincoln, "To Henry J. Raymond," November 28, 1860, *Collected Works*, 4:145–46; Lincoln, "To John A. Gilmer," December 15, 1860, *Collected Works*, 4:151–53.

3. Lincoln, "To Alexander H. Stephens," November 30, 1860, *Collected Works*, 4:146; Alexander H. Stephens, "Union Speech of 1860," Georgia Legislature, November 14, 1860, in *Confederate Records of the State of Georgia*, comp. Allen D. Candler (Atlanta: Chas. P. Bird, State Printer, 1909), 1:194–95, http://civilwarcauses.org/steph2.htm (accessed November 4, 2019).

4. Lincoln, "Fragment on the Constitution and the Union," [ca. January, 1861], Collected Works, 4:168–69; Georgia Declaration of Secession, January 29, 1861, http://www.civil-war.net/pages/georgia_declaration.asp (accessed November 4, 2019).

5. Lincoln, "Fragment on the Constitution and the Union," [ca. January, 1861], *Collected Works*, 4:169.

6. Ibid.

7. Ibid.

8. Stephen A. Douglas, December 30, 1845, speech quoted in Martin H. Quitt, *Stephen A. Douglas and Antebellum Democracy* (New York: Cambridge University Press, 2012), 94; Stephen A. Douglas, "Douglas at Chicago, July 9, 1858," in Angle, *Created Equal?* 12. For the most authoritative commentary on Douglas and popular sovereignty, see Jaffa, *Crisis of the House Divided*, chaps. 2 and 16.

9. Lincoln, "To John D. Defrees," December 18, 1860, *Collected Works*, 4:155.

10. Stephen A. Douglas, "The Dividing Line between Federal and Local Authority: Popular Sovereignty in the Territories," *Harper's New Monthly Magazine* 19, no. 112 (September 1859), 528. For the context of, and

reaction to, Douglas's article, see Christopher Childers, *The Failure of Popular Sovereignty: Slavery, Manifest Destiny, and the Radicalization of Southern Politics* (Lawrence: University Press of Kansas, 2012), 270–74.

11. Lincoln, "To Samuel Galloway," July 28, 1859, *Collected Works*, 3:394; Lincoln, "Autobiography Written for John L. Scripps" [ca. June, 1860], *Collected Works*, 4:67; Lincoln, "Speech at Peoria, Illinois," October 16, 1854, *Collected Works*, 2:255.

12. Lincoln, "Speech at Columbus, Ohio," September 16, 1859, *Collected Works*, 3:423; Lincoln, "Speech at New Haven, Connecticut," March 6, 1860, *Collected Works*, 4:18.

13. National Democratic (Breckenridge) Platform (1860), http://history. furman.edu/~benson/docs/bdemplat.htm (accessed November 4, 2019). For Douglas's refusal to endorse a federal slave code as the price of gaining the support of Southern Democrats in 1860, see his letter to Iowa newspaper editor J. B. Dorr (June 22, 1859), in *The Letters of Stephen A. Douglas*, ed. Robert W. Johannsen (Urbana: University of Illinois Press, 1961), 447.

14. Lincoln, "Fragment on the Constitution and the Union," [ca. January, 1861], *Collected Works*, 4:168–69; "South Carolina Ordinance of Secession," December 20, 1860, https://digital.scetv.org/teachingAmer history/lessons/Ordinance.htm (accessed November 4, 2019); "South Carolina Declaration of the Causes of Secession," 151.

15. Lincoln, "Speech at Peoria, Illinois," October 16, 1854, *Collected Works*, 2:274.

16. See Thomas Jefferson, "1776: Declaration of Independence (various drafts)," Online Library of Liberty, http://oll.libertyfund.org/pages /1776-declaration-of-independence-various-drafts.

17. Lincoln, "To Anton C. Hesing, Henry Wendt, Alexander Fisher, Committee," June 30, 1858, *Collected Works*, 2:475. See also Don E. Fehrenbacher, *Prelude to Greatness: Lincoln in the 1850's* (Stanford, CA: Stanford University Press, 1962), 6–7.

18. William Lloyd Garrison, *William Lloyd Garrison and the Fight against Slavery: Selections from* The Liberator, ed. William E. Cain (Boston: Bedford Books/St. Martin's Press, 1995), 87, 89, 101, 113–14, 115; Henry Mayer, *All on Fire: William Lloyd Garrison and the Abolition of Slavery* (New York: St. Martin's Press, 1998), 444–45.

19. Lincoln, "To Salmon P. Chase," June 9, 1859, *Collected Works*, 3:384; Lincoln, "To Schuyler Colfax," July 6, 1859, *Collected Works*, 3:391.

20. Lincoln, "To Schuyler Colfax," July 6, 1859, *Collected Works*, 3:391; Lincoln, "Second Debate with Stephen A. Douglas at Freeport, Illinois," August 27, 1858, *Collected Works*, 3:40, 41. See also Lincoln, "To Alonzo J. Grover," January 15, 1860, *Collected Works*, 3:514.

21. Stephen A. Douglas, "First Debate with Stephen A. Douglas at Ottawa, Illinois," August 21, 1858, *Collected Works*, 3:6.

22. Lincoln, "Address before the Young Men's Lyceum of Springfield, Illinois," January 27, 1838, *Collected Works*, 1:112, 111. See also Jon D. Schaff, *Lincoln and the Limits of Liberal Democracy: Statesmanship and Presidential Power* (Carbondale: Southern Illinois University, 2019), esp. chap. 1.

23. Lincoln, "To Williamson Durley," October 3, 1845, *Collected Works*, 1:348.

24. Lincoln, "To Duff Green," December 28, 1860, *Collected Works*, 4:162; Lincoln, "Seventh and Last Debate with Stephen A. Douglas at Alton, Illinois," October 15, 1858, *Collected Works*, 3:311; Lincoln, "Message to Congress in Special Session," July 4, 1861, *Collected Works*, 4:434.

25. Lincoln, "First Inaugural Address," March 4, 1861, *Collected Works*, 4:263; Lincoln, "Reply to Emancipation Memorial Presented by Chicago Christians," September 13, 1862, *Collected Works*, 5:424.

26. Lincoln, "To Horace Greeley," August 22, 1862, *Collected Works*, 5:388.

27. Ibid., 5:389; Lincoln, "To Albert G. Hodges," April 4, 1864, *Collected Works*, 7:281; Francis Carpenter, "The Emancipation Proclamation: Interesting Sketch of Its History by the Artist," *New York Times*, June 16, 1865, col. 4, 1.

28. James K. Polk, "Veto Message," *House Journal*, 30th Cong., 1st sess., December 15, 1847, 82–98, https://memory.loc.gov/cgi-bin/query/r?ammem /hlaw:@field(DOCID+@lit(hj0439)) (accessed November 4, 2019).

29. Lincoln, "Speech in United States House of Representatives on Internal Improvements," June 20, 1848, *Collected Works*, 1:488; U.S. Const., art. VI, cl. 2.

30. Lincoln, "To Duff Green," December 28, 1860, *Collected Works*, 4:162, 163n1; Lincoln, "First Inaugural Address," March 4, 1861, *Collected Works*, 4:270. For the Corwin amendment's legislative development and eventual passage by Congress, though it failed to be ratified, see Michael Vorenberg, *Final Freedom: The Civil War, the Abolition of Slavery, and the Thirteenth Amendment* (New York: Cambridge University Press, 2001), 20–22; Christian G. Samito, *Lincoln and the Thirteenth Amendment* (Carbondale: Southern Illinois University Press, 2015), 21–26.

31. Lincoln, "Response to a Serenade," February 1, 1865, *Collected Works*, 8:254, 255; Lincoln, "Speech at Peoria, Illinois," October 16, 1854, *Collected Works*, 2:270; Lincoln, "Emancipation Proclamation," January 1, 1863, *Collected Works*, 6:29.

32. Lincoln, "To Erastus Corning and Others," [June 12,] 1863, *Collected Works*, 6:264. For a discussion of Lincoln's cultivation of popular opinion, see Allen C. Guelzo, "'Public Sentiment Is Everything': Abraham

Lincoln and the Power of Public Opinion," in *Lincoln and Liberty: Wisdom for the Ages*, ed. Lucas E. Morel (Lexington: University Press of Kentucky, 2014), 171–90.

33. Lincoln, "Message to Congress in Special Session," July 4, 1861, *Collected Works*, 4:429–30. For Attorney General Edward Bates's confirmation of the legitimacy of Lincoln's habeas suspension, see "Suspension of the Privilege of the Writ of Habeas Corpus," 10 Op. Att'y Gen. 74 (July 5, 1861). See also James A. Dueholm, "Lincoln's Suspension of the Writ of Habeas Corpus: An Historical and Constitutional Analysis," *Journal of the Abraham Lincoln Association* 29, no. 2 (Summer 2008): 47–66.

34. Lincoln, "Speech at Peoria, Illinois," October 16, 1854, *Collected Works*, 2:275.

4. Lincoln and Slavery: An Appeal to the Founders' Compromise

1. Lincoln, "Speech at Elwood, Kansas," December 1 [November 30?], 1859, *Collected Works*, 3:496; Lincoln, "Speech at Edwardsville, Illinois," September 11, 1858, *Collected Works*, 3:92, 93.

2. Lincoln, "Speech at Springfield, Illinois," June 26, 1857, *Collected Works*, 2:406.

3. Stephen A. Douglas, "Douglas at Chicago, July 9, 1858," in Angle, *Created Equal?* 23. See also Stephen A. Douglas, "First Debate with Stephen A. Douglas at Ottawa, Illinois," August 21, 1858, *Collected Works*, 3:10; Robert W. Johannsen, *Stephen A. Douglas* (New York: Oxford University Press, 1973), 96–111.

4. Lincoln, "Speech at Chicago," July 10, 1858, *Collected Works*, 2:500.

5. Lincoln, "To George Robertson," August 15, 1855, *Collected Works*, 2:318; Lincoln, "Definition of Democracy," [August 1, 1858?], *Collected Works*, 2:532.

6. Lincoln, "Fragment on Slavery," [April 1, 1854?], *Collected Works*, 2:222–23.

7. Lincoln, "Fragment on Pro-Slavery Theology," [October 1, 1858?], *Collected Works*, 3:205; Lincoln, "Speech at Peoria, Illinois," October 16, 1854, *Collected Works*, 2:271.

8. John C. Calhoun, "Speech on the Reception of Abolition Petitions," delivered in the Senate, February 6, 1837, in *Union and Liberty: The Political Philosophy of John C. Calhoun*, ed. Ross M. Lence (Indianapolis: Liberty Fund, 1992), 474; Lincoln, "Speech at Springfield, Illinois," June 26, 1857, *Collected Works*, 2:409.

9. Lincoln, "To Henry L. Pierce and Others," April 6, 1859, *Collected Works*, 3:376.

10. Thomas Jefferson, *Notes on the State of Virginia*, "Query XVIII: Manners," *Portable Thomas Jefferson*, 215.

11. Lincoln, "To Henry L. Pierce and Others," April 6, 1859, *Collected Works*, 3:376; Lincoln, "Speech at Springfield, Illinois," July 17, 1858, *Collected Works*, 2:518; Lincoln, "Speech at Chicago, Illinois," July 10, 1858, *Collected Works*, 2:493–94; Lincoln, "Speech at Columbus, Ohio," September 16, 1859, *Collected Works*, 3:410; Lincoln, "Fragment of a Speech" [ca. December 28, 1857], *Collected Works*, 2:451–52. For background on Lincoln's 1859 speeches in Ohio, see Gary Ecelbarger, "Before Cooper Union: Abraham Lincoln's 1859 Cincinnati Speech and Its Impact on His Nomination," *Journal of the Abraham Lincoln Association* 30, no. 1 (Winter 2009): 1–17.

12. Lincoln, "Protest in Illinois Legislature on Slavery," March 3, 1837, *Collected Works*, 1:75.

13. Lincoln, "To Joshua F. Speed," August 24, 1855, *Collected Works*, 2:320.

14. Ibid., 2:323.

15. Lincoln, "To George Robertson," August 15, 1855, *Collected Works*, 2:318.

16. Republican Party Platform of 1860 (May 1860), https://teachingamerican history.org/library/document/republican-party-platform-1860/ (accessed November 5, 2019); Stephen A. Douglas, "Douglas at Springfield, July 17, 1858," in Angle, *Created Equal?* 55.

17. For a useful exposition of prudence as a signature element of Lincoln's statesmanship, see Joseph R. Fornieri, *Abraham Lincoln, Philosopher Statesman* (Carbondale: Southern Illinois University Press, 2014), chap. 2; Lincoln, "Speech at Chicago, Illinois," July 10, 1858, *Collected Works*, 2:492.

18. Lincoln, "To Schuyler Colfax," July 6, 1859, *Collected Works*, 3:390–91; Lincoln, "Fourth Debate with Stephen A. Douglas at Charleston, Illinois," September 18, 1858, *Collected Works*, 3:181.

19. Lincoln, "Notes for Speeches at Columbus and Cincinnati, Ohio" [September 16, 17, 1859], *Collected Works*, 3:430.

20. Lincoln, "Speech at Chicago, Illinois," July 10, 1858, *Collected Works*, 2:492.

21. Ibid.

22. Lincoln, "Speech at Springfield, Illinois," July 17, 1858, *Collected Works*, 2:520; Harry V. Jaffa, *A New Birth of Freedom: Abraham Lincoln and the Coming of the Civil War* (Lanham, MD: Rowman & Littlefield, 2000), 227. See also Jaffa, *Crisis of the House Divided*, 370.

23. Lincoln, "Speech at Springfield, Illinois," July 17, 1858, *Collected Works*, 2:520–21; Lincoln, "Speech at Lewistown, Illinois," August 17, 1858, *Collected Works*, 2:546 (emphasis added).

24. Lincoln, "Speech at Springfield, Illinois," July 17, 1858, *Collected Works*, 2:514, 515.

25. Lincoln, "Seventh and Last Debate with Stephen A. Douglas at Alton, Illinois," October 15, 1858, *Collected Works*, 3:306, 313.

26. Lincoln, "To Elihu B. Washburne," December 13, 1860, *Collected Works*, 4:151; Lincoln, "Speech at Peoria, Illinois," October 16, 1854, *Collected Works*, 2:275, 276.

27. Lincoln, "Speech at New Haven, Connecticut," March 6, 1860, *Collected Works*, 4:22.

28. "The Great Seal of the United States," U.S. Department of State, Bureau of Public Affairs (July 2003), https://2009-2017.state.gov/documents /organization/27807.pdf (accessed November 5, 2019).

5. Lincoln and Original Intent: An Appeal to the Founders' Relevance

1. Douglas, "Dividing Line between Federal and Local Authority," 519–37. For Lincoln's most direct rebuttal of the *Harper's* essay, see Lincoln, "Speech at Columbus, Ohio," September 16, 1859, *Collected Works*, 3:400–425.

2. Lincoln, "Address at Cooper Institute, New York City," February 27, 1860, *Collected Works*, 3:522.

3. Ibid., 3:534–35. See also Lincoln, "Fragments: Notes for Speeches," [ca. September, 1859?], *Collected Works*, 3:398–99.

4. Lincoln, "Fragment on Slavery," [April 1, 1854?], *Collected Works*, 2:222.

5. Lincoln, "Speech in United States House of Representatives on Internal Improvements," June 20, 1848, *Collected Works*, 1:488.

6. Lincoln, "Speech at Leavenworth, Kansas," December 3, 1859, *Collected Works*, 3:501.

7. See Irving R. Kaufman, "What Did the Founding Fathers Intend?" *New York Times Magazine*, February 23, 1986; cf. Harry V. Jaffa, "What Were the 'Original Intentions' of the Framers of the Constitution of the United States?" *University of Puget Sound Law Review* 10 (1987): 351–95.

8. Dred Scott v. Sanford (1857), 60 U.S. 393, 407–9.

9. Ibid., 409–10.

10. Ibid., 426.

11. Ibid.; Lincoln, "Speech at Springfield, Illinois," June 26, 1857, *Collected Works*, 2:400–403.

12. Lincoln, "Speech at Springfield, Illinois," June 26, 1857, *Collected Works*, 2:403, 401, 400–404. For a comparison of Lincoln and Taney on the proper interpretation of the founders' understanding of slavery, see Thomas L. Krannawitter, "Who Was Right about the Founding, Lincoln or Taney?" chap. 3 in *Vindicating Lincoln: Defending the Politics of Our Greatest President* (Lanham, MD: Rowman & Littlefield, 2008).

13. Stephen A. Douglas, "Douglas at Chicago, July 9, 1858," in Angle, *Created Equal?* 21, 20; Lincoln, "First Debate with Stephen A. Douglas at Ottawa, Illinois," August 21, 1858, *Collected Works*, 3:28.

14. Lincoln, "Speech at Springfield, Illinois," June 26, 1857, *Collected Works*, 2:400–402; Lincoln, "Address before the Young Men's Lyceum of Springfield, Illinois," January 27, 1838, *Collected Works*, 1:112.

15. Lincoln, "First Inaugural Address," March 4, 1861, *Collected Works*, 4:268; Lincoln, "Speech at Cincinnati, Ohio," September 17, 1859, *Collected Works*, 3:460. For a modern Lincolnian approach to Supreme Court jurisprudence, see John Agresto, *The Supreme Court and Constitutional Democracy* (Ithaca, NY: Cornell University Press, 1984).

16. Lincoln, "Second Inaugural Address," March 4, 1865, *Collected Works*, 8:333. See also Lucas E. Morel, "Of Justice and Mercy in Abraham Lincoln's Second Inaugural Address," *American Political Thought*, vol. 4 (Summer 2015), 455–66.

17. Lincoln, "To John B. Fry," August 15, 1860, *Collected Works*, 4:95; Lincoln, "To August Belmont," July 31, 1862, *Collected Works*, 5:350. See Allen C. Guelzo, *Lincoln's Emancipation Proclamation: The End of Slavery in America* (New York: Simon & Schuster, 2004), 229–32. Cf. Vorenberg, *Final Freedom*, 41–48, 107–14, 123–27.

18. Attorney General Edwin Meese III, "Speech before the American Bar Association," Washington, DC, July 9, 1985, https://fedsoc.org/commentary/publications/the-great-debate-attorney-general-ed-meese-iii-july-9-1985 (accessed November 5, 2019).

19. Justice William J. Brennan Jr., "Speech to the Text and Teaching Symposium at Georgetown University," Washington, DC, October 12, 1985, https://fedsoc.org/commentary/publications/the-great-debate-justice-william-j-brennan-jr-october-12-1985 (accessed November 5, 2019).

20. Ibid. Justice Brennan quoted Justice Robert Jackson's concurring opinion in Brown v. Allen (1953), 344 U.S. 443, 540.

21. Stephen A. Douglas, "First Debate with Stephen A. Douglas at Ottawa, Illinois," August 21, 1858, *Collected Works*, 3:12, 10.

22. Stephen A. Douglas, "Third Debate with Stephen A. Douglas at Jonesboro, Illinois," September 15, 1858, *Collected Works*, 3:112; Stephen A. Douglas, "First Debate with Stephen A. Douglas at Ottawa, Illinois," August 21, 1858, *Collected Works*, 3:12; Stephen A. Douglas, "Fourth Debate with Stephen A. Douglas at Charleston, Illinois," September 18, 1858, *Collected Works*, 3:178; Stephen A. Douglas, "Second Debate with Stephen A. Douglas at Freeport, Illinois," August 27, 1858, *Collected Works*, 3:55.

23. Lincoln, "First Debate with Stephen A. Douglas at Ottawa, Illinois," August 21, 1858, *Collected Works*, 3:19; Lincoln, "Speech at Peoria,

Illinois," October 16, 1854, *Collected Works*, 2:276; Confederate Constitution, art. I, sec. 9, cl. 4, quoted in James R. Stoner Jr., "The Case of the Confederate Constitution," in *The Political Thought of the Civil War*, ed. Alan Levine, Thomas W. Merrill, and James R. Stoner Jr. (Lawrence: University Press of Kansas, 2018), 283.

24. Lincoln, "Message to Congress in Special Session," July 4, 1861, *Collected Works*, 4:429. For discussion of Lincoln's interpretation of the habeas corpus provision, see Benjamin A. Kleinerman, *The Discretionary President: The Promise and Peril of Executive Power* (Lawrence: University Press of Kansas, 2009); Daniel Farber, *Lincoln's Constitution* (Chicago: The University of Chicago Press, 2003).

25. Lincoln, "Message to Congress in Special Session," July 4, 1861, *Collected Works*, 4:430–31.

26. For Attorney General Edward Bates's report, issued the day after Lincoln's "Message to Congress in Special Session," see "Suspension of the Privilege of the Writ of Habeas Corpus," 10 Op. Att'y Gen. 74 (July 5, 1861). See also Dueholm, "Lincoln's Suspension of the Writ of Habeas Corpus," 47–66.

27. Lincoln, "Message to Congress in Special Session," July 4, 1861, *Collected Works*, 4:435, 426.

28. For an examination of original intent that focuses on a free people's intention to govern themselves constitutionally, see William B. Allen, "The Constitution: Not Just a Law—A Dissent from Misspelled Original Intent," *Derailing the Constitution: The Undermining of American Federalism*, ed. Edward B. McLean (Wilmington, DE: ISI Books, 1997), 61–85.

Conclusion: Lincoln as Conservative Liberal or Liberal Conservative?

1. Lincoln, "Address at Cooper Institute, New York City," February 27, 1860, *Collected Works*, 3:537.

2. William H. Herndon and Jesse W. Weik, *Herndon's Lincoln*, ed. Douglas L. Wilson and Rodney O. Davis (Urbana: University of Illinois Press, 2006), 363.

3. Lord Godfrey Rathbone Benson Charnwood, *Lincoln: A Biography*, intro. Peter W. Schramm (1917; repr., Lanham, MD: Madison Books, 1996), 18.

4. Lincoln, "Eulogy on Henry Clay," July 6, 1852, *Collected Works*, 2:126; Lincoln, "Annual Message to Congress," December 1, 1862, *Collected Works*, 5:537.

5. Lincoln, "Resolutions in Behalf of Hungarian Freedom," January 9, 1852, *Collected Works*, 2:115; Lincoln, "Reply to Lorenzo Montufar," April 24, 1862, *Collected Works*, 5:198.

6. Lincoln, "Reply to Joseph Bertinatti," July 30, 1864, *Collected Works*, 7:473; Lincoln, "Address at Cooper Institute, New York City," February 27, 1860, *Collected Works*, 3:550.

7. William Jefferson Clinton, "First Inaugural Address," January 20, 1993, United States Presidents' Inaugural speeches: From Washington to George W. Bush, https://www.gutenberg.org/files/925/925-h/925-h .htm#link2H_4_0053 (accessed November 5, 2019).

8. Martin Luther King Jr., "I See the Promised Land," April 3, 1968, in *I Have a Dream: Writings and Speeches That Changed the World*, ed. James Melvin Washington (New York: HarperCollins, 1992), 197; King, "I Have a Dream," August 28, 1963, ibid., 102.

9. "Interview with Alexander W. Randall and Joseph T. Mills," August 19, 1864, *Collected Works*, 7:508.

BIBLIOGRAPHY

Agresto, John. *The Supreme Court and Constitutional Democracy*. Ithaca, NY: Cornell University Press, 1984.

Allen, Danielle. *Our Declaration: A Reading of the Declaration of Independence in Defense of Equality*. New York: W. W. Norton, 2014.

Allen, William B. "The Constitution: Not Just a Law—A Dissent from Misspelled Original Intent." In *Derailing the Constitution: The Undermining of American Federalism*, edited by Edward B. McLean, 61–85. Wilmington, DE: ISI Books, 1997.

Angle, Paul M., ed. *Created Equal? The Complete Lincoln-Douglas Debates of 1858*. 1958. Reprint, Chicago: Midway, 1985.

Bailey, Jeremy D. *Thomas Jefferson and Executive Power*. New York: Cambridge University Press, 2007.

Bailyn, Bernard. *The Ideological Origins of the American Revolution*. Cambridge, MA: Harvard University Press, 1967.

Bicknell, John. *Lincoln's Pathfinder: John C. Fremont and the Violent Election of 1856*. Chicago: Chicago Review Press, 2017.

Bray, Robert. *Reading with Lincoln*. Carbondale: Southern Illinois University Press, 2010.

Brennan, William J., Jr. "Speech to the Text and Teaching Symposium at Georgetown University," Washington, DC, October 12, 1985. https://fedsoc.org/commentary/publications/the-great-debate-justice-william-j-brennan-jr-october-12-1985.

Brookhiser, Richard. *Founders' Son: A Life of Abraham Lincoln*. New York: Basic Books, 2014.

Buchanan, James. "State of the Union Address," December 3, 1860. https://teachingamericanhistory.org/library/document/1860-state-of-the-union-address/.

Burlingame, Michael. *Abraham Lincoln: A Life*. 2 vols. Baltimore: Johns Hopkins University Press, 2008.

Byron, Lord. "Personal, Lyric, and Elegiac Ode to Napoleon Buonaparte." In *Poetry of Byron, Chosen and Arranged by Matthew Arnold*. London: Macmillan, 1881. Bartleby.com, 2013. https://www.bartleby.com/205/31.html.

Calhoun, John C. "Speech on the Reception of Abolition Petitions," delivered in the Senate, February 6, 1837. In *Union and Liberty: The Political Philosophy of John C. Calhoun*, edited by Ross M. Lence, 461–76. Indianapolis: Liberty Fund, 1992.

Calhoun, Samuel W., and Lucas E. Morel. "Abraham Lincoln's Religion: The Case for His Ultimate Belief in a Personal, Sovereign God." *Journal of the Abraham Lincoln Association* 33, no. 1 (Winter 2012): 38–74.

Cameron, Simon. Form Letter of the Secretary of War to State Governors, April 15, 1861. *The Civil War and Northwest Wisconsin* (blog), https://thecivilwarandnorthwestwisconsin.wordpress.com/2011/04/15/1861-april-15-lincolns-call-for-troops/.

Carpenter, Francis. "The Emancipation Proclamation: Interesting Sketch of Its History by the Artist." *New York Times*, June 16, 1865, col. 4, 1.

Ceaser, James W. "The First American Founder." *National Affairs* 36 (Summer 2018). https://www.nationalaffairs.com/publications/detail/the-first-american-founder.

Charnwood, Lord Godfrey Rathbone Benson. *Lincoln: A Biography*. Introduction by Peter W. Schramm. 1917. Reprint, Lanham, MD: Madison Books, 1996.

Childers, Christopher. *The Failure of Popular Sovereignty: Slavery, Manifest Destiny, and the Radicalization of Southern Politics*. Lawrence: University Press of Kansas, 2012.

Clinton, William Jefferson. "First Inaugural Address," January 20, 1993. United States Presidents' Inaugural Speeches: From Washington to George W. Bush. https://www.gutenberg.org/files/925/925-h/925-h.htm#link2H_4_0053.

Douglas, Stephen A. "The Dividing Line between Federal and Local Authority: Popular Sovereignty in the Territories." *Harper's New Monthly Magazine* 19, no. 112 (September 1859): 519–37.

———. "Invasion of States" Speech. *Congressional Globe* (January 23, 1860), 554, col. 2.

Dueholm, James A. "Lincoln's Suspension of the Writ of Habeas Corpus: An Historical and Constitutional Analysis." *Journal of the Abraham Lincoln Association* 29, no. 2 (Summer 2008): 47–66.

Ecelbarger, Gary. "Before Cooper Union: Abraham Lincoln's 1859 Cincinnati Speech and Its Impact on His Nomination." *Journal of the Abraham Lincoln Association* 30, no. 1 (Winter 2009): 1–17.

———. *The Great Comeback: How Abraham Lincoln Beat the Odds to Win the 1860 Republican Nomination*. New York: St. Martin's Press, 2008.

Farber, Daniel. *Lincoln's Constitution*. Chicago: University of Chicago Press, 2003.

Fehrenbacher, Don E. *Prelude to Greatness: Lincoln in the 1850's*. Stanford, CA: Stanford University Press, 1962.

Fornieri, Joseph R. *Abraham Lincoln, Philosopher Statesman*. Carbondale: Southern Illinois University Press, 2014.

Garrison, William Lloyd. *William Lloyd Garrison and the Fight against Slavery: Selections from* The Liberator. Edited by William E. Cain. Boston: Bedford Books/St. Martin's Press, 1995.

Georgia Declaration of Secession, January 29, 1861. http://www.civil-war
.net/pages/georgia_declaration.asp.

Guelzo, Allen C. *Lincoln and Douglas: The Debates That Defined America*.
New York: Simon & Schuster, 2008.

———. *Lincoln's Emancipation Proclamation: The End of Slavery in America*.
New York: Simon & Schuster, 2004.

———. "'Public Sentiment Is Everything': Abraham Lincoln and the Power
of Public Opinion." In *Lincoln and Liberty: Wisdom for the Ages*, edited by
Lucas E. Morel, 171–90. Lexington: University Press of Kentucky, 2014.

Herndon, William H. *Herndon on Lincoln: Letters*. Edited by Douglas L.
Wilson and Rodney O. Davis. Urbana: Knox College Lincoln Studies
Center and the University of Illinois Press, 2016.

Herndon, William H., and Jesse W. Weik. *Herndon's Lincoln*. Edited by
Douglas L. Wilson and Rodney O. Davis. Urbana: University of Illinois
Press, 2006.

Holzer, Harold. *Lincoln at Cooper Union: The Speech That Made Abraham
Lincoln President*. New York: Simon & Schuster, 2004.

Howe, Daniel Walker. "Why Abraham Lincoln Was a Whig." *Journal of the
Abraham Lincoln Association* 16, no. 1 (Winter 1995): 27–39.

Jaffa, Harry V. *Crisis of the House Divided: An Interpretation of the Issues
in the Lincoln-Douglas Debates*. 1959. Reprint, Chicago: University of
Chicago Press, 1982.

———. *A New Birth of Freedom: Abraham Lincoln and the Coming of the
Civil War*. Lanham, MD: Rowman & Littlefield, 2000.

———. "What Were the 'Original Intentions' of the Framers of the Constitution of the United States?" *University of Puget Sound Law Review*
10 (1987): 351–448.

Jefferson, Thomas. *The Portable Thomas Jefferson*. Edited by Merrill D. Peterson. New York: Penguin Books, 1975.

———. "1776: Declaration of Independence (various drafts)." Online Library of Liberty. http://oll.libertyfund.org/pages/1776-declaration-of
-independence-various-drafts.

———. *The Writings of Thomas Jefferson*. Edited by H. A. Washington. 9
vols. New York: J. C. Riker, 1853–55.

Johannsen, Robert W., ed. *The Letters of Stephen A. Douglas*. Urbana: University of Illinois Press, 1961.

———. *Stephen A. Douglas*. New York: Oxford University Press, 1973.

Kaufman, Irving R. "What Did the Founding Fathers Intend?" *New York
Times Magazine*, February 23, 1986.

Keyssar, Alexander. *The Right to Vote: The Contested History of Democracy in
the United States*. Rev. ed. 2000. Reprint, New York: Basic Books, 2009.

King, Martin Luther, Jr. *I Have a Dream: Writings and Speeches That Changed the World*. Edited by James Melvin Washington. New York: Harper-Collins, 1992.

Kleinerman, Benjamin A. *The Discretionary President: The Promise and Peril of Executive Power*. Lawrence: University Press of Kansas, 2009.

Knox, Henry. "From Brigadier General Henry Knox," November 26, 1777. In *The Papers of George Washington*, Revolutionary War Series, vol. 12, *October 1777–December 1777*, edited by Frank E. Grizzard Jr. and David R. Hoth, 414–17. Charlottesville: University of Virginia Press, 2002.

Krannawitter, Thomas L. *Vindicating Lincoln: Defending the Politics of Our Greatest President*. Lanham, MD: Rowman & Littlefield, 2008.

Lincoln, Abraham. *The Collected Works of Abraham Lincoln*. Edited by Roy P. Basler. 9 vols. New Brunswick, NJ: Rutgers University Press, 1953–55.

"Lincoln and New Jersey: A Bicentennial Tribute by the New Jersey State Archives." State of New Jersey Department of State, 2011. http://www.nj.gov/state/archives/lincoln.html.

Locke, John. *Second Treatise of Government* [1690]. Edited by C. B. Macpherson. Indianapolis: Hackett, 1980.

Maier, Pauline. *American Scripture: Making the Declaration of Independence*. New York: Alfred A. Knopf, 1997.

Malanson, Jeffrey J. "The Founding Fathers and the Election of 1864." *Journal of Abraham Lincoln Association* 36, no. 2 (Summer 2015): 1–25.

Mayer, David N. *The Constitutional Thought of Thomas Jefferson*. Charlottesville: University Press of Virginia, 1994.

Mayer, Henry. *All on Fire: William Lloyd Garrison and the Abolition of Slavery*. New York: St. Martin's Press, 1998.

Meese, Edwin, III. "Speech before the American Bar Association," Washington, DC, July 9, 1985. https://fedsoc.org/commentary/publications/the-great-debate-attorney-general-ed-meese-iii-july-9-1985.

Merrill, Thomas W. "The Later Jefferson and the Problem of Natural Rights." In *The Political Thought of the Civil War*, edited by Alan Levine, Thomas W. Merrill, and James R. Stoner Jr., 27–44. Lawrence: University Press of Kansas, 2018.

Morel, Lucas E. "Lincoln, Race, and the Spirit of '76." *Perspectives in Political Science* 39, no. 1 (2010): 3–11.

———. "Of Justice and Mercy in Abraham Lincoln's Second Inaugural Address." *American Political Thought* 4 (Summer 2015): 455–66.

Nabors, Forrest A. *From Oligarchy to Republicanism: The Great Task of Reconstruction*. Columbia: University of Missouri Press, 2017.

National Democratic (Breckenridge) Platform, 1860. http://history.furman.edu/~benson/docs/bdemplat.htm.

Oakes, James. *Freedom National: The Destruction of Slavery in the United States, 1861–1865*. New York: W. W. Norton, 2012.

Polk, James K. "Veto Message." *House Journal*, 30th Cong., 1st sess., December 15, 1847, 82–98. https://memory.loc.gov/cgi-bin/query/r?ammem /hlaw:@field(DOCID+@lit(hj0439)).

Quitt, Martin H. "In the Shadow of the Little Giant: Lincoln before the Great Debates," *Journal of the Abraham Lincoln Association* 36, no. 1 (Winter 2015): 18–46.

———. *Stephen A. Douglas and Antebellum Democracy*. New York: Cambridge University Press, 2012.

Republican Party Platform of 1860, May 1860. https://teachingamerican history.org/library/document/republican-party-platform-1860/.

Samito, Christian G. *Lincoln and the Thirteenth Amendment*. Carbondale: Southern Illinois University Press, 2015.

Schaff, Jon D. *Lincoln and the Limits of Liberal Democracy: Statesmanship and Presidential Power*. Carbondale: Southern Illinois University, 2019.

Schaub, Diana. "Lincoln and the Daughters of Dred Scott: A Reflection on the Declaration of Independence." In *When in the Course of Human Events: 1776 at Home, Abroad, and in American Memory*, edited by Will R. Jordan, 189–210. Macon, GA: Mercer University Press, 2018.

Soodalter, Ron. *Hanging Nathaniel Gordon: The Life and Trial of an American Slave Trader*. New York: Atria, 2006.

"South Carolina Declaration of the Causes of Secession," December 24, 1860. In *The Civil War: The First Year Told by Those Who Lived It*, edited by Brooks D. Simpson, Stephen W. Sears, and Aaron Sheehan-Dean, 149–55. Washington, DC: Library of America, 2011.

"South Carolina Ordinance of Secession," December 20, 1860. https://digital .scetv.org/teachingAmerhistory/lessons/Ordinance.htm.

Stephens, Alexander H. "Union Speech of 1860," Georgia Legislature, November 14, 1860. In Allen D. Candler, comp., *Confederate Records of the State of Georgia*, vol. 1, 183–205. Atlanta: Chas. P. Byrd, State Printer, 1909

Stoner, James R., Jr. "The Case of the Confederate Constitution." In *The Political Thought of the Civil War*, edited by Alan Levine, Thomas W. Merrill, and James R. Stoner Jr., 273–90. Lawrence: University Press of Kansas, 2018.

Taylor, Zachary. "Inaugural Address," March 5, 1849. http://avalon.law.yale .edu/19th_century/taylor.asp.

United States Congress, March 1, 1784, Printed Resolution on Western Territory Government; with Notations by Thomas Jefferson. Thomas Jefferson Papers at the Library of Congress, Manuscript Division. http://hdl.loc .gov/loc.mss/mtj.mtjbib000873.

U.S. Department of State, Bureau of Public Affairs, July 2003, "The Great Seal of the United States." https://2009-2017.state.gov/documents/organization /27807.pdf.

Van Buren, Martin. "First Inaugural Address," March 4, 1837. https://www .gutenberg.org/files/925/925-h/925-h.htm#link2H_4_0013.

Vorenberg, Michael. *Final Freedom: The Civil War, the Abolition of Slavery, and the Thirteenth Amendment*. New York: Cambridge University Press, 2001.

Washington, George. *George Washington: A Collection*. Edited by W. B. Allen. Indianapolis: Liberty Fund, 1988.

Watson, Bradley C. S. *Living Constitution, Dying Faith: Progressivism and the New Science of Jurisprudence*. Wilmington, DE: ISI Books, 2009.

Webster, Daniel. *The Bunker Hill Monument, Adams and Jefferson: Two Orations*. Boston: Houghton, Mifflin, 1893. https://archive.org/stream /bunkerhillmonum01websgoog#page/n6/mode/2up.

Weems, Mason L. *The Life of Washington*. Introduction by Peter S. Onuf. New York: Routledge, 1996.

White, Jonathan W. *Abraham Lincoln and Treason in the Civil War: The Trials of John Merryman*. Baton Rouge: Louisiana State University Press, 2011.

Wilson, Douglas L. *Lincoln's Sword: The Presidency and the Power of Words*. New York: Alfred A. Knopf, 2006.

Wilson, Woodrow. "The Author and Signers of the Declaration," September 1907. In *Woodrow Wilson: The Essential Political Writings*, edited by Ronald J. Pestritto, 97–105. Lanham, MD: Lexington Books, 2005.

Winkle, Kenneth. *The Young Eagle: The Rise of Abraham Lincoln*. Dallas: Taylor, 2001.

INDEX

Lucas E. Morel is professor of politics and head of the Politics Department at Washington and Lee University, and an Honored Visiting Graduate Professor in the master of arts program in American history and government at Ashland University in Ohio. His previous publications include *Lincoln and Liberty: Wisdom for the Ages* and *Lincoln's Sacred Effort: Defining Religion's Role in American Self-Government.* He is a trustee of the Supreme Court Historical Society, a former president of the Abraham Lincoln Institute, and a member of the U.S. Semiquincentennial Commission, which will plan activities to commemorate in 2026 the founding of the United States of America.

CONCISE
LINCOLN
LIBRARY

This series of concise books fills a need for short studies of the life, times, and legacy of President Abraham Lincoln. Each book gives readers the opportunity to quickly achieve basic knowledge of a Lincoln-related topic. These books bring fresh perspectives to well-known topics, investigate previously overlooked subjects, and explore in greater depth topics that have not yet received book-length treatment. For a complete list of current and forthcoming titles, see www.conciselincolnlibrary.com.

Other Books in the Concise Lincoln Library